WILLIAMS-SONOMA

# MASTERING

# Frozen Desserts

Author
**MELANIE BARNARD**

General Editor
**CHUCK WILLIAMS**

Photographer
**MARK THOMAS**

NEW YORK · LONDON · TORONTO · SYDNEY

# Contents

# About this book

*Mastering Frozen Desserts* offers every reader a cooking class in book form, a one-on-one lesson with a seasoned teacher standing by your side, explaining each recipe step-by-step—with plenty of photographs to illustrate every detail.

From a simple scoop of ice cream to an old-fashioned banana split to an elegant multilayered torte, frozen desserts are both varied and versatile, with something to appeal to everyone.

Here's how this book comprises a complete introductory course on frozen desserts: It begins with descriptions of the ice creams, gelatos, sorbets, granitas, and composed frozen desserts that you will be making, along with guidelines on preparing, flavoring, and freezing; information on ingredients; and ideas for serving and storing. Next comes the Basic Recipes chapter, which includes sauces, whipped cream, and a simple cookie that doubles as a serving dish. It is followed by an illustrated techniques chapter that will teach you fourteen key skills, from how to temper eggs to how to chop chocolate. The Ice Cream & Gelato chapter provides instructions for several easy-to-make favorites, from the classic French vanilla and a spice-laced pumpkin ice cream to a vibrant green pistachio-studded gelato. In the Sorbet & Granita chapter, you are carefully guided through the steps for making such dairy-free desserts as mango sorbet and watermelon granita. Finally, all your newly acquired knowledge is put to work when you turn to the recipes in Composed Frozen Desserts, where you'll learn to combine different elements to create a wide variety of special-occasion desserts.

With *Mastering Frozen Desserts* beside you, you'll soon be making many different ice creams, gelatos, and other favorite frozen desserts with ease.

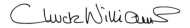

# Working with the Recipes

Spending a lazy summer afternoon slowly churning a batch of ice cream, and then licking the smooth, rich result from the paddle, is a tradition that belongs to a simpler time. This book will help you discover some of that old fashioned pleasure. In it you will learn how to choose the ingredients and use the equipment necessary to produce a wide range of frozen desserts, creating memorable finales for both family suppers and dinner parties.

Most frozen desserts require only a few everyday ingredients—cream, sugar, eggs, and fruit or other flavorings—but understanding how to combine them makes all the difference in the final result. This book is the next best thing to having an experienced cooking teacher with you, showing you the way.

First, you will learn about the various types of frozen desserts offered in this book, including French custard-style ice cream, Italian gelato, refreshing sorbet, mild sherbet, and icy granita.

The subsequent recipe chapters each begin with a master recipe that leads you through the preparation of each type of frozen dessert, usually followed by six variations and a trio of serving ideas. Start with these skill-building recipes; the easy-to-follow instructions and clear, step-by-step photos will provide you with a solid foundation of learning. After you progress through the master recipes, try some of the other recipes in the chapters. Secure in the knowledge you have gained, your confidence will blossom.

In addition to providing an extensive curriculum in frozen desserts, this book gives you dozens of ways to put your newly acquired skills to practice. For example, once you master French Vanilla Ice Cream (page 47), you will be ready to tackle Strawberry Ice Cream (page 54), or you will be able to stack the ice cream with other ingredients to make Tiramisu Ice Cream Torte (page 118).

For tips about how to stock your kitchen with basic cake-making tools and equipment, turn to pages 130-133.

# Types of Frozen Desserts

Frozen desserts embrace a multitude of offerings that are enjoyed in some form in almost every culture. In the pages ahead you will learn how to make smooth, custard-based ice creams and gelatos; dairy-based sherbets; mouth-watering sorbets; cooling granitas, and the more refined composed frozen desserts. All of them rely on a handful of simple components that are adjusted to create different flavors and textures.

## Ice Cream, Gelato & Sherbet

The term *ice cream* is descriptive of its basic makeup: iced or frozen cream—or milk and cream—sweetened with sugar. Philadelphia-style ice cream is made from an uncooked base that does not include eggs. It is quick to prepare and easy to put together. French-style ice cream is made from a cooked egg custard that must be chilled before churning. It calls for a little more skill and some advance planning.

Gelato, arguably the best loved of Italian desserts, is made with less cream than French-style ice cream. Less air is incorporated during churning, resulting in a more intense flavor and denser texture. Nut-and-chocolate and other rich gelatos are stand-alone desserts, needing no sauces or other adornments.

Sherbet is a cross between ice cream and sorbet. Usually made with a fruit purée and sugar, it sometimes contains milk as well. Because of its lower butterfat content, the consistency of sherbet is icier and coarser than ice cream.

## Sorbet & Granita

Sorbet is the result of incorporating air into a sweet purée while churning and freezing it. It contains no eggs or dairy products—nothing to dilute the intense flavor of the main ingredient, which is usually fruit.

The difference between sorbet and granita is that sorbet is churned in an ice cream maker, resulting in a smooth, fluffy texture, while granita is simply frozen in a pan and stirred or scraped by hand to produce a dessert with an icy consistency. A granita can be made with almost any liquid, including coffee, an herb-infused syrup, or a fruit juice or purée. Part of the appeal of sorbet and granita comes from their bright, vivid color, and colorful and flavorful liqueurs or syrups are often added.

## Composed Desserts

Composed desserts are frozen creations that are typically shaped in molds or more simply layered. Each recipe calls for elements and techniques that you will have learned throughout this book. They are the creations that invariably impress when you serve them. Many of the most elaborate frozen desserts, such as the dramatic Individual Baked Alaskas (page 113) and the over-the-top Banana Split (page 129), require minimal last minute preparation. Others, such as the elegant Tiramisu Ice Cream Torte (page 118) and crunchy Ice Cream Sandwiches (page 123), are completely finished ahead of time and can wait in the freezer for up to a day before they are plated and presented at the table.

# Ingredients for Frozen Desserts

The basic ingredients used for making frozen desserts are typically few, and some of them may already be in your refrigerator or pantry. Every ingredient contributes both flavor and texture to the dessert, which means that you must choose all of them carefully. Always buy the best-quality and freshest eggs, milk, and cream that you can find, and use fresh fruits only when they are in season and at their most abundant and luscious.

### Dairy & Eggs

Milk, cream, and eggs, the most common components of a custard base, are the backbone of most ice creams and gelatos.

Milk is sold in a variety of butterfat contents. Look for whole milk, which has the most amount of butterfat (a minimum of 3.25 percent) and the sweetest flavor. When shopping for heavy (double) cream, which has a butterfat content of between 36 and 40 percent, look for a pasteurized product. Ultrapasteurized cream, which has a longer shelf life, is more commonly available, but pasteurized cream tastes better and whips up thicker when used for whipped cream.

Buy low-fat or whole-milk buttermilk, rather than nonfat for the recipes in this book, for the ideal flavor and texture, and be sure to shake the container vigorously before pouring to recombine the liquid and solids.

Grade A large eggs were used to test the recipes in this book. Using larger or smaller eggs will affect the body and richness of the finished dessert.

Mascarpone, an Italian triple-cream cheese, can be used to make ice cream bases richer and more flavorful.

### Sweeteners

A number of different types of sweeteners are used in the making of frozen desserts. Granulated sugar is comprised of small white crystals that dissolve easily in liquid when heated, or after a few minutes of stirring or beating in liquid at room temperature. Do not use superfine (caster) or confectioners' (icing) sugar as a

substitute. Brown sugar contains molasses, which gives it color, moisture, and a subtle flavor.

Molasses, a by-product of sugar refining, comes in three types, but only light molasses is called for in this book. Either sulfured (lighter tasting) or unsulfured can be used. Corn syrup is a thick liquid made by processing cornstarch (cornflour) with enzymes or acids. Light corn syrup is clear, while dark syrup has caramel color and flavor added. Both are used to increase the silkiness of flavored syrups.

## Fruits & Flavorings

Fruits and flavorings give frozen desserts their distinctive flavor and personality. Buy fresh fruit only if it is in season, and sample the fruit before adding it to the ice cream to make sure it is flavorful. When fresh fruits are unavailable, frozen fruits are acceptable substitutes. Try to buy unsweetened varieties.

Freshly ground whole spices have the most potent flavor. Preground spices should be stored in a cool, dark place and used within a few months.

Coffee beans that are freshly ground and then brewed yield a wonderful flavor, but dissolved instant espresso also works well in many recipes.

Chopped nuts add extra flavor and texture to ice cream and gelato. For a more subtle nut flavor, steep the nuts in the custard and then strain them out.

Using flaked coconut and canned coconut milk yields a more consistent flavor than using a fresh coconut.

Extracts (essences) provide a little sweetness along with flavor to desserts. Always buy extracts that are labelled "pure," never the imitation varieties.

Add liqueurs only in small amounts, as they can overpower the taste of the ice cream. If a recipe calls for a non-alcoholic syrup, look for a naturally flavored brand for the best taste.

## Chocolate & Cocoa Powder

Always purchase the best-quality chocolate products that you can afford. Semisweet (plain) and bittersweet chocolate are often interchangeable, but since ice cream is naturally sweet, bittersweet chocolate, which contains less sugar, is preferred for the recipes in this book. Cocoa powder is available in two types: regular (nonalkalinized) and Dutch process (alkalinized). Either can be used for the recipes in this book, but Dutch-process, which is treated with an alkali solution, provides a richer, deeper taste and darker color.

# Preparing, Flavoring & Freezing Frozen Desserts

Good-tasting, well-textured ice creams and other frozen desserts depend not only on high-quality ingredients, but also on a solid understanding of how to flavor, churn, freeze, and store them. The basic techniques are included in the master recipes in this book, so that once you have perfected these recipes, such as the French Vanilla Ice Cream on page 47, you will be able to apply your knowledge to making scores of other frozen desserts.

When learning to make frozen desserts, as with most skills, practice makes perfect. For example, if you have never cooked a custard before, you might need a few tries before you master the smooth consistency that freezes into a velvety ice cream. In time, your patience will be rewarded with homemade ice cream that is just as delicious as any that you will find at the store.

### Mise en Place

*Mise en place,* French for "everything in its place," is a principal rule of all good cooking. Essentially, it calls for readying your ingredients and tools before you begin to make a recipe so you will be calm and focused as you work. You don't want to have to stop to chop chocolate before you can add it to your just-off-the-heat custard base.

Before starting a recipe, read it from beginning to end, making a list of the ingredients and equipment you will need at the same time. Be sure also to read the instruction book that came with your

ice cream maker, so that you know how it works. Arrange the ingredients and equipment in the order they will be used. Prepare them in a logical order as well. For example, if both citrus zest and juice are needed, grate the zest from the fruit first, and then squeeze the juice, straining out the seeds.

### Measuring Ingredients

Dry and liquid measuring cups and spoons, and sometimes a kitchen scale, are needed for making frozen desserts. Granulated sugar and other dry ingredients are measured by spooning them into the measuring cup to the brim, and then leveling the top using the a thin metal spatula or back or a table knife.

To measure brown sugar, scoop it into a dry measuring cup, then tamp it down with your fingers or the back of spoon. Add more sugar until it is tightly packed and level with the rim of the cup.

Most liquid ingredients are easy to measure by spooning or pouring, but some are trickier. Sticky liquids such

as molasses and corn syrup cling to the sides of the measuring cup, making them difficult to measure accurately. If you lightly coat the cup with oil before pouring in the syrup, the syrup will pour out freely and cleanly.

### Flavoring Frozen Desserts

Milk, cream, sugar, and sometimes eggs are the "body" of frozen desserts, but flavorings form the fashionable dress that gives them a personality. Like good clothing, flavors should be added with care, at the correct time, and often in different layers.

Too much of a good thing, even chocolate, can overwhelm the flavor of a frozen dessert or impair its texture. Liqueurs and liquors are pleasing flavor enhancers, but their alcohol content lowers the freezing point of a liquid—and an excess will prevent it from freezing at all—so don't be tempted to add more than the recipe indicates.

The ability to layer flavors—adding the same flavor at different times or in different forms, as well as combining complementary flavors—is the mark of a knowledgeable cook. Layering flavors is especially important when making frozen desserts, since intense cold mutes flavors. It is always a good idea to allow most frozen desserts to sit for a few minutes at room temperature before serving.

The best sorbets and granitas are good examples of flavor layering. Raspberry Sorbet (page 87) contains both puréed raspberries and raspberry liqueur or syrup, as well as a small quantity of lemon juice, an ingredient often added to fruit desserts to brighten their flavor. Orange and Lemon Sorbets (page 86) and Pink Grapefruit Granita (page 96) contain both grated zest and fruit juice to intensify their flavor. The fresh mint in Mint Granita (page 97) is paired with green crème de menthe to boost the flavor.

Ice creams can also be enhanced by layering flavors. Coconut Ice Cream (page 53) benefits from the richness of coconut milk and the crunch of flaked coconut. Strawberry Ice Cream (page 54) gets its flavor from both puréed strawberries in the custard and freshly sliced strawberry bits scattered throughout the ice cream.

Chocolate is an excellent layering ingredient. All chocolate is made from cocoa beans, but various types of chocolate differ depending on how the beans are processed. Chocolate Ice Cream (page 59) and Chocolate Sorbet (page 88) both have unsweetened cocoa (for depth) and bittersweet chocolate (for richness), while Chocolate–Chocolate Chip Ice Cream (page 61) adds a third layer with the chips, which add a quick dose of chocolate crunch.

### Ice Cream Accompaniments

Though ice cream is delicious without embellishment, a simple tuile cookie (page 22) formed into an edible dish or served as a crunchy adornment is a nice addition. If you purchase cookies for ice cream sandwiches, seek out high-quality cookies with a crisp texture to contrast with the smooth ice cream.

Other accompaniments, such as dessert sauces and whipped cream, can also be purchased if you don't have time to make them. Check labels carefully and choose products that have the shortest shelf life and contain the freshest ingredients.

Vanilla, like chocolate, also comes from an aromatic bean. The purest and most intense vanilla flavor is achieved by using the vanilla bean, and especially the tiny black seeds found inside of it. To extract the maximum amount of flavor, add the pod and its seeds to the liquid ingredients at the beginning of the cooking process; the heat and the time the pod spends steeping in liquid will concentrate the flavor. Before freezing the custard, strain out the pod but leave the tiny seeds. They add visual interest along with additional flavor. Some ice creams, especially those that do not use a cooked base or that contain vanilla as a secondary flavor, call for vanilla extract (essence). Because pure vanilla extract is alcohol based, always add it after the ingredients are cooked, so that it doesn't evaporate and the heat doesn't diminish its flavor.

Certain ingredients, many of which are also paired in nature, form classic combinations. Coffee intensifies the flavor of chocolate, and both are tropical beans. Likewise, vanilla deepens the flavor of both coffee and chocolate, and is an integral ingredient in almost all forms of sweetened chocolate. Coconut and tropical fruits grow together in warm climates, and they pair well in serving ideas, such as Mango-Coconut Bonbon Sundae (page 85). Other combinations are so familiar that we would think it odd to use one ingredient without the other. Pumpkin and other fall fruits such as apples are almost always partnered with heady cool-weather spices such as cinnamon, ginger, and cloves. Pumpkin Ice Cream (page 65) and Spiced Cider Granita (page 97) are good examples of this tradition.

A contrast of textures and temperatures also characterizes many frozen desserts. Slipping soft ice cream between crisp cookies to make sandwiches (page 123) is an American favorite, as is baked Alaska (page 113), in which ice cream sits on a dense-crumbed cake round and is enclosed in an oven-singed meringue, in a perfect marriage of hot and cold. Other contrasting textures include filling crisp choux pastries with ice cream and served with warm, smooth chocolate sauce for Profiteroles (page 107), while in Tiramisu Ice Cream Torte (page 118), layers of silky mascarpone and espresso ice creams are separated by a layer of rich chocolate sauce, then surrounded with a stack with cakelike ladyfingers. Finally, crisp dark chocolate coats creamy vanilla ice cream in traditional Ice Cream Bars (page 126).

## Churning Frozen Desserts

The most important devices in freezing frozen desserts are your ice cream maker and freezer. The ice cream makers that are available today are far more advanced and easier to use than their old-fashioned hand-cranked counterparts. Offered in a wide variety of shapes and sizes from those designed for home use to the more elaborate machines for professional operations, ice cream machines are now electrically powered so all you have to do is pour in the custard and the machine will do the rest. Unless your ice cream maker has a built-in freezer unit, you will need to freeze the mixing container in advance. If you have room in your freezer, you can leave it there at all times so that it is always ready. Just be sure you dry it completely before you store it in the freezer, and cover it with a plastic bag to prevent ice crystals from forming. Different manufacturers have different instructions, so be sure to read the instruction manual that comes with your machine carefully before beginning.

Custard-based ice creams and gelatos are churned in an ice-cream maker and take little time to prepare, but require advance planning. Cooked custards must be chilled for optimal freezing and the best flavor development.

Take care when adding spirits of any kind to ice-cream bases. Alcohol lowers the freezing point, and too much will prevent the ice cream from setting properly. Be sure to use only the amount indicated in the recipe, or the finished product won't harden fully.

You need to follow a few rules when adding ingredients to churned ice cream. Use small bittersweet or semisweet (plain) chocolate chips, which will melt in the mouth easily. Larger chips tend to freeze solid, making them difficult to chew. If using marshmallows, use soft, fresh ones that have enough moisture to keep them chewy and soft in the ice cream; otherwise, they will freeze solid.

Almost any nut, from pecans to peanuts to pistachios, can be used. Untoasted nuts have a bit more moisture and meld into the ice cream better than toasted nuts.

Dried fruits such as cranberries work well, and can be added while the mixture is churning. Be sure the fruit pieces are small, or they will harden too much. Fresh fruits such as strawberries and peaches can also be added during churning, but be sure to cut them into small pieces as large chunks tend to freeze too hard and will become tasteless.

### Food Safety

Use a clean work surface and utensils when chopping and mixing the ingredients to prevent bacterial contamination. Uncooked eggs can carry salmonella, but the bacteria will be killed if the custard base is heated to 160°F (71°C) during cooking. If you are in doubt, test the custard with an instant-read thermometer. The egg whites in the meringue for Individual Baked Alaskas (page 113) may not be fully cooked, so if you are concerned about safety, check your market's refrigerated egg section, or look for pasteurized egg whites or meringue powder on the shelf. Keep dairy products of all types refrigerated until ready to use, and always chill warm foods such as custards quickly and thoroughly after cooking.

# Serving Frozen Desserts

Once you have finished making your ice cream or other frozen dessert, you will want to serve it with some style. Your choices are varied, from simply scooping it into an elegant dish, balancing it on top of a sugar cone, or nestling it alongside a slice of birthday cake to fashioning it into a layered torte. You can also dress it up with a sauce or whipped cream or decorate it with fruit or a dusting of sugar.

Some of the best serving ideas are the simplest. You can scoop ice cream or other frozen desserts into almost any small dish, bowl, or goblet. Chopped nuts or fruits, sauces, and Sweetened Whipped Cream (page 30) are perfect adornments. Or, you can rest ice cream, gelato, or sherbet in the top of a crisp sugar cone. And when you really want to treat yourself, make an all-American Banana Split (page 129).

Ice cream can also be an integral part of a more elaborate dessert, such as Individual Baked Alaskas (page 113) or Frozen Key Lime Soufflé (page 101). In these desserts, the ice cream has to be softened slightly so that it can be spread in a mold. The best way to soften it is to transfer it from the freezer to the refrigerator, where it will slowly soften until it can be easily spread.

Slice tortes and bombes as soon as you remove them from the freezer, but let the slices stand for a few minutes so that they can warm slightly and soften, which will make them easier for the diner to eat.

An attractive way to decorate a serving is to first dust the empty plate with confectioners' (icing) sugar or unsweetened cocoa, using a fine-mesh sieve or metal shaker, and then to put the frozen dessert on the dusted plate. You can spoon sauces over or around ice cream, gelato, or sorbet, or pipe them in decorative patterns by squeezing them through the cut-off tip of a sandwich-sized plastic bag. Drag a toothpick through the piped sauce to create a swirled or zigzag design.

# Storing Frozen Desserts

Knowing the best way to store frozen desserts and their ingredients is an important part of learning how to make frozen desserts. Ingredients must be kept properly for them to deliver their maximum flavor. The desserts themselves are extremely sensitive to heat and should always be kept very cold until serving time, and then left out at room temperature for only a few minutes before they are served.

Because homemade ice creams, gelatos, sherbets, and sorbets have no added emulsifiers or stabilizers, they can be served right after their initial freezing. Served immediately after churning, they will have a silky smooth consistency (much like soft-serve ice cream) that will be too soft for scooping. They will also have a milder flavor, since frozen desserts need a few hours in the freezer to "ripen" and develop a good, deep flavor and an optimal texture. It is best to plan ahead and store frozen desserts in the freezer for a few hours before you serve them.

Custard-based ice creams and gelatos are at their best when served 6 to 12 hours after freezing. After 3 days, they can form ice crystals and become grainy.

Philadelphia-style ice creams and sherbets don't have a custard base to preserve them, so they won't keep as long. They should be eaten within 2 days.

Ice creams and gelatos with fresh fruit chunks will start to spoil quicker than other ice creams. They should also be eaten within 2 days.

Because sorbets and granitas do not contain any dairy products to preserve them, they will quickly start to dilute and form ice crystals. They are best eaten within 24 hours.

Frozen desserts with added elements, such as meringue or ladyfingers, should not be stored in the freezer for more than an hour after they have been assembled. If kept longer, the meringue will start to *weep*, or form water droplets, and the cakelike ladyfingers will get soggy from the moisture in the ice cream. To keep your dessert from being marred or damaged by other objects in the freezer, place toothpicks in the top and then cover with a sheet of plastic wrap and carefully store in a flat part of the freezer.

Store frozen desserts in tightly covered containers in the part of the freezer that is the most consistently cold. Do not keep them near the freezer door, where they may partially thaw and refreeze each time the door is opened. Though you can freeze desserts in the mixing container of some ice cream makers, it is better to transfer them to a freezer-safe plastic or metal container with an airtight lid. Place a piece of plastic wrap (don't use foil, which will stick to the surface) directly on the surface of the ice cream, gelato, sherbet, or sorbet to help prevent freezer burn. Use a container that holds the ice cream snugly. Too much air will cause ice crystals to form.

Refreeze softened ice cream quickly, and serve within 24 hours. Once ice cream has slightly melted, it will lose the air churned into it, and it will develop "freezer burn" or become icy when refrozen.

# Creating Your Own Frozen Desserts

You can create many wonderful frozen desserts, from sodas to sundaes, by combining just a few different elements. Here are some recipes to get you started. You can use them as inspiration to come up with your own ideas, too, mixing and matching other recipes you find in the book. The ice cream, sorbet, sherbet, and granita amounts are given in scoops. Each scoop is equal to ½ cup or 4 ounces (48 g).

MALTS, SHAKES & SODAS

| | KEY COMPONENTS | PREPARATION |
|---|---|---|
| **Chocolate Malt**<br>Makes 1 large or<br>2 small shakes | 2 scoops Chocolate Ice Cream (page 59), ¼ cup (2 fl oz/60 ml) room-temperature Chocolate Sauce (page 24), ¾ cup (6 fl oz/180 ml) milk, and ¼ cup (¾ oz/20 g) chocolate malted milk powder. | Add all of the ingredients to a blender along with 1 cup (8 oz/125 g) crushed ice cubes. Blend until smooth, 30–45 seconds. If the shake is too thick, add more milk, if it is too thin, add more ice cubes and blend until smooth. Pour into 1 tall glass or divide between 2 small glasses. |
| **Strawberry Shake**<br>Makes 1 large or<br>2 small shakes | 2 scoops Strawberry Ice Cream (page 54), ¾ cup (6 fl oz/180 ml) whole milk, and ½ cup (2 oz/60 g) strawberries. | Add all of the ingredients to a blender along with 1 cup (8 oz/125 g) crushed ice cubes. Blend until smooth, 30–45 seconds. Pour into 1 tall glass or divide between 2 small glasses. |
| **Mocha Ice Cream Soda**<br>Makes 4 sodas | 8 scoops Espresso Ice Cream (page 52), 2 cups (16 fl oz/500 ml) chilled club soda or seltzer water, and ½ cup (4 fl oz/125 ml) warm Chocolate Sauce (page 24). | Put 2 scoops of the ice cream into each of 4 tall glasses. Fill each glass with club soda. Add the sauce, dividing evenly, and stir with a spoon. Let sit for 2 minutes to allow the soda water to froth up a bit. Serve right away. |

PARFAITS

| | KEY COMPONENTS | PREPARATION |
|---|---|---|
| **Double Chocolate Parfait**<br>Makes 4 parfaits | 8 scoops Chocolate Sorbet (page 88), 1 cup (8 fl oz/250 ml) room-temperature Chocolate Sauce (page 24), and 1 cup (8 fl oz/250 ml) Sweetened Whipped Cream (page 30). | For each parfait, place 1 scoop sorbet into a tall, footed dessert glass. Add 2 tablespoons sauce and then 2 tablespoons whipped cream. Repeat the layers. |
| **Chocolate Walnut Parfait**<br>Makes 4 parfaits | 1 cup (4 oz/125 g) chopped walnuts, 8 scoops French Vanilla Ice Cream (page 47), and 1 cup (8 fl oz/250 ml) room-temperature Chocolate Sauce (page 24). | For each parfait, place 2 tablespoons walnuts into a tall, footed dessert glass. Add 1 scoop ice cream and then 2 tablespoons sauce. Repeat the layers. |
| **Sorbet Parfait**<br>Makes 4 parfaits | 8 scoops any flavor sorbet (pages 81–88) and 2 cups (16 fl oz/500 ml) Sweetened Whipped Cream (page 30). | For each parfait, place 1 scoop sorbet into a tall, footed dessert glass. Add ¼ cup (2 fl oz/60 ml) whipped cream. Repeat the layers. |
| **Granita Parfait**<br>Makes 4 parfaits | 8 scoops any flavor granita (pages 91–97) and 2 cups (16 fl oz/500 ml) Sweetened Whipped Cream (page 30). | For each parfait, place 1 scoop granita into a tall, footed dessert glass. Add ¼ cup (2 fl oz/60 ml) whipped cream. Repeat the layers. |

| | KEY COMPONENTS | PREPARATION |
|---|---|---|
| **Classic Hot Fudge Sundae**<br>Makes 4 sundaes | 8 scoops French Vanilla Ice Cream (page 47), 1 cup (8 fl oz/250 ml ) warm Chocolate Sauce (page 24), 1 cup (8 fl oz/250 ml) Sweetened Whipped Cream (page 30), and ½ cup (2 oz/60 g) chopped nuts. | For each sundae, put 2 scoops ice cream into a sundae dish and then pour ¼ cup (2 fl oz/60 ml) sauce over the top. Add whipped cream and sprinkle with 2 tablespoons nuts. |
| **Triple Chocolate Sundae**<br>Makes 4 sundaes | 4 scoops White Chocolate Gelato (page 74), 1 cup (8 fl oz/250 ml) warm Chocolate Sauce (page 24), 4 scoops Chocolate–Chocolate Chip Ice Cream (page 61), 1 cup (8 fl oz/250 ml) Sweetened Whipped Cream (page 30), and 6 tablespoons Chocolate Curls (page 37). | For each sundae, put 1 scoop gelato into a sundae dish and pour 3 tablespoons sauce over the top. Add 1 scoop ice cream and drizzle with 1 tablespoon sauce. Top with ¼ cup (2 fl oz/60 ml) whipped cream and garnish with 1½ tablespoons chocolate curls. |
| **Cookies-and-Cream Sundae**<br>Makes 4 sundaes | 4 scoops French Vanilla Ice Cream (page 47), 4 tuile cookie cups (page 22), 1 cup (8 fl oz/250 ml) Chocolate, Caramel, or Butterscotch Sauce (pages 24–28), and 1 cup (3 oz/90 g) crushed Tuile Cookies (page 22). | For each sundae, put 1 scoop ice cream into a tuile cup. Top with ¼ cup (2 fl oz/60 ml) of the sauce of your choice, and sprinkle with ¼ cup (¾ oz/20 g) of the crushed cookies. |
| **Caramel-Nut Sundae**<br>Makes 4 sundaes | 8 scoops Caramel Ice Cream (page 53), 1 cup (8 fl oz/250 ml) warm Caramel Sauce (page 26), and 6 tablespoons (2 oz/60 g) crushed store-bought nut brittle. | For each sundae, put 2 scoops ice cream into a sundae dish. Drizzle with ¼ cup (2 fl oz/60 ml) sauce and sprinkle with 1½ tablespoons crushed nut brittle. |
| **Butterscotch Sundae**<br>Makes 4 sundaes | 8 scoops Buttermilk Sherbet (page 77) or Orange Sorbet (page 86) and 1 cup (8 fl oz/250 ml) warm Butterscotch Sauce (page 28). | For each sundae, put 2 scoops sherbet or sorbet into a sundae dish. Spoon ¼ cup (2 fl oz/60 ml) sauce over the top. |
| **Espresso-Cream Sundae**<br>Makes 4 sundaes | 8 scoops French Vanilla Ice Cream (page 47), 1 cup (8 fl oz/250 ml) hot brewed espresso (page 37), 1 cup (8 fl oz/250 ml) Sweetened Whipped Cream (page 30), and 4 store-bought chocolate-covered coffee beans, optional. | For each sundae, put 2 scoops ice cream into a sundae dish. Pour ¼ cup (2 fl oz/60 ml) espresso over the top, and top with ¼ cup (2 fl oz/60 ml) whipped cream. Garnish with a chocolate-covered coffee bean, if you like. |
| **Raspberry Sundae**<br>Makes 4 sundaes | 4 scoops Buttermilk Sherbet (page 77), 4 scoops Mango Sorbet (page 81), 4 scoops Peach Sorbet (page 86), and 1 cup (8 fl oz/250 ml) Raspberry Purée (page 117). | For each sundae, put 1 scoop sherbet and 1 scoop of each sorbet into a sundae dish. Drizzle ¼ cup (2 fl oz/60 ml) purée over the top. |
| **Turtle Bar Sundae**<br>Makes 4 sundaes | 4 Ice Cream Bars (page 126) without the sticks, ½ cup (4 fl oz/125 ml) Butterscotch Sauce (page 28), and 6 tablespoons crushed pecans. | For each sundae, put 1 bar onto a shallow dish. Top with 2 tablespoons sauce and sprinkle with 2 tablespoons pecans. |

# 1

# Basic Recipes

Sauces and other toppings are the finishing touches for many frozen desserts. On the following pages, you will learn how to make such popular sauces as chocolate, caramel, and butterscotch. You'll also find a recipe for tuile cookies, which can be shaped into a serving cup or offered as an accompaniment, and for whipped cream, the perfect topping for nearly any dessert.

Canola oil nonstick cooking spray, optional

4 tablespoons (2 oz/60 g) unsalted butter, cut into 4 equal pieces

2 large egg whites (page 34)

½ cup (4 oz/125 g) granulated sugar

½ teaspoon vanilla extract (essence)

¼ teaspoon almond extract (essence)

⅓ cup (2 oz/60 g) all-purpose (plain) flour

½ cup (2 oz/60 g) sliced (flaked) almonds

MAKES 12–18 COOKIES (3–4 INCHES/ 7.5–10 CM)

**PASTRY CHEF'S TIP**

*If you do not have a silicone liner, lightly coat the baking sheet with canola oil nonstick cooking spray. Sift 1 tablespoon all-purpose (plain) flour evenly over the surface, and then invert the sheet to remove any excess flour. Use a shiny metal pan; a dark one will cause the cookies to brown too quickly.*

# Tuile Cookies

When these warm almond-flecked cookies are draped over a rolling pin, they resemble the curved roof tiles that give them their name (*tuiles* means "tiles" in French). You can also bake them as flat wafers to accompany scoops of ice cream, or you can shape them into edible bowls to hold the scoops.

## 1 Preheat the oven and assemble the equipment

Position a rack in the middle of the oven so the cookies will be evenly surrounded with heat, and preheat to 375°F (190°C). Line a 10-by-15-by-1-inch (25-by-38-by-2.5-cm) rimmed baking sheet with a silicone baking liner. Decide what shape you want the final cookies to be. If you want to shape them into tiles, coat a dowel-shaped rolling pin with the canola oil spray. If you want to shape the cookies into small bowls, coat the outside of six ¾ cup (6–fl oz/180-ml) ceramic ramekins with the nonstick spray. If you are serving them flat, no extra equipment is needed. Have ready a large wire rack for cooling the cookies. Because the cookies will harden quickly as they cool, be sure to have all your equipment ready before the cookies come out of the oven.

## 2 Melt the butter and mix the ingredients

Put the butter pieces in a small saucepan and place over low heat. When the butter is melted and as soon as you see the butter turn pale brown, remove it from the heat. Be careful to not let the butter burn. Let the brown butter cool to room temperature, about 5 minutes. Meanwhile, in a small bowl, use a whisk to mix the egg whites with the cooled melted butter, sugar, and vanilla and almond extracts until the mixture is frothy and opaque. Add the flour and whisk until the mixture is smooth and forms a thin, creamy batter, about 1 minute.

## 3 Portion the batter

Using a measuring tablespoon, scoop a heaping spoonful of the batter from the mixing bowl and drop onto the prepared baking sheet, spacing the cookies at least 4 inches (10 cm) apart. The batter will spread a lot during baking.

## 4 Top the cookies with almonds

Sprinkle the top of each scoop of batter with 4 or 5 almond slices, spacing them so that the almonds do not overlap each other (this would hinder shaping the cookies after they are baked).

## 5 Bake the cookies

Place the baking sheet in the preheated oven. Bake the cookies until they have spread into thin wafers, the edges are dark gold, and the centers are pale gold in color, 6–8 minutes. (The centers of the cookies will still look moist.) Rotate the baking sheet halfway through the baking time to ensure even baking (in case some areas of your oven are hotter than others, known as *hot spots*).

## 6 Shape the cookies

Remove the cookies from the oven and immediately use a thin metal spatula (you need a thin spatula because the cookies are very thin and fragile) to remove them, one at a time, from the baking sheet. If you are planning to leave them flat, simply transfer the cookies to the rack immediately to cool. For curved cookies, drape them over the prepared rolling pin and shape with hands. For cookie cups, place the warm cookies over the prepared inverted ramekins, gently molding them to the shape of the ramekin. If the cookies harden on the baking sheet before you are able to shape them, return the baking sheet to the oven for about 30 seconds to soften the cookies again. As soon as the cookies are cool and set, remove them from the rolling pin or ramekin and carefully transfer them to the wire rack to cool completely. Repeat the baking and molding process with the remaining batter, scooping, baking, and forming the cookies in batches as necessary. Bake only 1 sheet at a time so the cookies will still be warm when you try to mold them.

## 7 Store the cookies

Use the cookies right away, or store the completely cooled cookies in a sturdy airtight container between layers of waxed paper. The cookies are very fragile, so handle and store them carefully. They will keep at room temperature for about 5 days, or wrapped tightly and frozen for about 1 month.

**PASTRY CHEF'S TIP**
*You can flavor this basic batter in many ways, such as adding 1 teaspoon grated orange or lemon zest or about ¼ teaspoon ground cinnamon or cloves or freshly grated nutmeg. Instead of sprinkling the cookies with sliced almonds, you can stir the same amount of chopped almonds or hazelnuts (filberts) right into the batter.*

# Chocolate Sauce

Buy the best chocolate you can afford, as its flavor will determine the success of this popular sauce. Served warm, room temperature, or cold, the chocolate flavor is deepened by the brown sugar and enriched with the heavy cream. It takes just minutes to make but keeps for weeks.

8 oz (250 g) bittersweet or semisweet (plain) chocolate

⅓ cup (3 oz/90 g) light corn syrup

¼ cup (2 oz/60 g) firmly packed light brown sugar

¾ cup (6 fl oz/180 ml) heavy (double) cream

1 teaspoon vanilla extract (essence)

MAKES ABOUT 2 CUPS (16 FL OZ/500 ML)

## 1 Chop the chocolate

If you need help chopping chocolate, turn to page 36. Place the chocolate on a cutting board. Grasp the handle of a serrated knife or chef's knife with one hand and, with your other hand placed about midpoint on the back of the blade, cut the chocolate into medium-sized chunks. (You don't want to touch the chocolate with your hand, as it could cause it to melt prematurely.) Then, move your hand closer to the tip of the blade and, using a rocking motion, cut the chocolate into even pieces. Be sure the pieces are small so that they will melt quickly. Put the chopped chocolate in a small heatproof bowl and set aside.

## 2 Heat the sugar and cream mixture

Put the corn syrup and brown sugar in a 1½-quart (1½-l) saucepan. Place the pan over medium-low heat and stir the mixture with a wooden spoon until the sugar is dissolved and the mixture is bubbling, 2–3 minutes. Stir in the cream and increase the heat to medium. Cook, continuing to stir, until the mixture is smooth, large bubbles form around the edges, and the mixture begins to foam up in the center, 3–4 minutes. Do not remove it from the heat until it foams up. If you do, the brown sugar may not dissolve thoroughly, and you will end up with a sauce that is not completely smooth.

## 3 Pour the hot mixture over the chocolate

Remove from the heat and, protecting your hands and arms with oven mitts and working slowly and carefully, immediately pour the hot mixture over the chocolate in the bowl, covering the chocolate with the liquid. Let the mixture stand without stirring for about 2 minutes to allow the chocolate to soften.

### 4 Stir in the vanilla extract

Add the vanilla extract (vanilla extract, which contains alcohol, is added at the end of the cooking process in order to preserve its flavor, which would dissipate if added to a hot mixture at the beginning of the heating process) and gently stir with the wooden spoon until the chocolate is melted and the sauce is shiny and smooth, 1–2 minutes.

### 5 Use or store the sauce

This sauce is thick and nearly firm when cold, making it a good choice for filling an ice cream torte. It is thick but spoonable at room temperature for layering in parfaits. When warm, it is easily pourable but also clings a bit to ice cream, making it the perfect hot fudge sauce. To serve the sauce right away, let it cool until it is lukewarm and then ladle over ice cream. Or, let it cool to room temperature, pour into a covered container, and store in the refrigerator for up to 1 week. The sauce can also be poured into an airtight container, covered tightly, and frozen for up to 1 month.

### 6 Warm or reheat the sauce, if needed

To use refrigerated sauce at room temperature, remove the container from the refrigerator and let it stand for about 1 hour. Or, if the sauce is frozen, thaw it in the refrigerator for at least 6 hours, then let it stand at room temperature for about 1 hour. To reheat the sauce, place the desired quantity in a small saucepan over very low heat and warm, stirring often, until it is lukewarm, 3–4 minutes. Do not let it boil, which could burn the chocolate and turn the sauce grainy and bitter.

**PASTRY CHEF'S TIP**

*Corn syrup will cling to a measuring cup, making it difficult to pour it all out. But experienced bakers know that lightly coating the cup with vegetable oil or nonstick cooking spray will make the contents, whether corn syrup, honey, or molasses, flow out more easily.*

# Caramel Sauce

Caramel is sugar that has been melted and cooked to change its color and flavor. Here, it is enriched with cream and flavored with vanilla to create a potent, deep amber topping for a variety of frozen desserts. The lemon juice heightens the overall flavor of the sauce, while the corn syrup gives it a nice sheen.

1 cup (8 oz/250 g) granulated sugar

2 tablespoons water

1 tablespoon light corn syrup

1 teaspoon fresh lemon juice

1 cup (8 fl oz/250 ml) heavy (double) cream, at room temperature

1 teaspoon vanilla extract (essence)

MAKES ABOUT 1½ CUPS (12 FL OZ/375 ML)

## 1 Combine the sugar, water, and corn syrup

If you need help caramelizing sugar, turn to page 38. Put the sugar, water, corn syrup, and lemon juice into a deep 1½- to 2-quart (1½- to 2-l) saucepan (the sauce will bubble up as it cooks, so make sure the pan is deep enough to keep it from bubbling over). Place the saucepan over medium heat and cook, stirring constantly with a long-handled wooden spoon, until the sugar is dissolved and the liquid is bubbling, and no grains of sugar are visible, 1–2 minutes. Make sure that the sugar is completely dissolved and the syrup is clear; even a small amount of undissolved sugar may prevent caramelization.

## 2 Simmer the caramel

Increase the heat to medium-high and bring the mixture to a gentle boil, occasionally stirring gently. Large bubbles should form all over the surface. If the mixture appears to be darkening unevenly, stir it gently or reduce the heat slightly to prevent scorching. Watch the mixture carefully. As soon as it turns a rich amber, after about 2–4 minutes, remove the pan from the heat. The mixture will continue to cook even when it is off the heat.

## 3 Add the cream

Protecting your hands and arms with oven mitts, and working slowly and carefully, immediately pour the cream into the hot syrup; this will stop the cooking. The hot syrup is likely to bubble up and splatter when you add the cream, so hold the pan away from you while you pour. The threat of bubbling up is another good reason to use a deep saucepan.

## 4 Stir the sauce and add the vanilla extract

Stir the sauce until smooth. If the mixture doesn't become perfectly smooth, place the saucepan over low heat and stir gently until smooth. Add the vanilla extract and stir to blend.

## 5 Use or store the sauce

Caramel sauce is a good topping for many frozen desserts. Use the sauce warm for topping pastries or sundaes, or at room temperature for garnishing ice cream sandwiches. (The sauce is thicker at room temperature than when it is warm.) To serve the sauce right away, let it cool until it is lukewarm and then ladle over ice cream. Or, let the sauce cool to room temperature, pour into a covered container, and store in the refrigerator for up to 1 week. The sauce can also be poured into an airtight container and frozen for up to 1 month.

## 6 Warm or reheat the sauce, if needed

To use refrigerated sauce at room temperature, remove the container from the refrigerator and let it stand for about 1 hour. Or, if the sauce is frozen, thaw it in the refrigerator for at least 6 hours, then let it stand at room temperature for about 1 hour. To reheat the sauce, place the desired quantity in a small saucepan over very low heat and warm, stirring often, until it is lukewarm, 3–4 minutes. Do not let it boil, which could burn the sauce.

**PASTRY CHEF'S TIP**

*If the caramel hardens and sticks to the bottom and sides of your saucepan, fill the pan three-fourths full of water, bring to a boil, and then pour it out. This will remove the hardened syrup and make the pan easier to clean.*

# Butterscotch Sauce

Butterscotch sauce is similar in color to Caramel Sauce (page 26), but it has an entirely different flavor. Brown sugar and dark corn syrup provide depth, cream and butter lend richness, and Scotch whiskey adds an intriguing sharpness. While the Scotch can be omitted, I like the contrast it imparts to this mixture.

1½ cups (10½ oz/330 g) firmly packed light brown sugar

½ cup (4 fl oz/125 ml) heavy (double) cream

4½ tablespoons (2¼ oz/70 g) unsalted butter, cut into small pieces

3 tablespoons dark corn syrup

2 tablespoons Scotch whiskey

1½ teaspoons vanilla extract (essence)

MAKES ABOUT 1½ CUPS (12 FL OZ/375 ML)

**PASTRY CHEF'S TIP**
*For a child-friendly version of this popular sundae topping, omit the Scotch and continue as directed. The taste will be slightly more mellow but still delicious.*

## 1 Melt the ingredients
Put the brown sugar, cream, butter, and corn syrup in a deep 1½- or 2-quart (1½- or 2-l) saucepan (the sauce will bubble up as it cooks, so it is important that the pan is deep enough that it won't bubble over). Place the saucepan over medium heat and cook, stirring constantly with a long-handled wooden spoon, until the sugar is dissolved and the liquid is bubbling, with no grains of sugar visible, 1–2 minutes.

## 2 Check for graininess
To test if the sugar is completely dissolved, spoon a small amount of the sauce onto a clean plate. Let cool for 1 minute and then run your finger through the sauce to see if the sugar crystals have dissolved. (Alternatively, lift up a syrup-coated wooden spoon to see if any grains of sugar are visible.) If the sauce feels or looks grainy instead of smooth, continue cooking and stirring for another minute and then test again.

## 3 Gently boil the sauce base
Increase the heat to medium-high and bring the sauce mixture to a gentle boil; there should be lots of bubbles at the edges of the pan and the center should rise and become somewhat foamy and bubbly. Stir often with the wooden spoon to prevent the mixture from scorching on the bottom. It's important to monitor the heat so the mixture doesn't boil over, so do not walk away from the stove. Be careful not to touch the sauce, as it will be very hot. Continue to boil and stir the sauce base until it is smooth and is thick enough to coat the back of the spoon when you lift it from the liquid, 4–5 minutes.

4 **Stir in the Scotch and vanilla extract**
Immediately remove the pan from the heat. Stir in the Scotch and the vanilla extract until the sauce is smooth. These ingredients, which both contain alcohol, are added after cooking because heat diminishes their flavor.

5 **Use or store the sauce**
Butterscotch sauce is a good topping for many frozen desserts. Use the sauce warm for topping pastries or at room-temperature for topping sundaes. (The sauce is thicker at room temperature than when it is warm.) To serve the sauce right away, let it cool until it is lukewarm and then ladle over ice cream. Or, let the sauce cool to room temperature, pour into a covered container, and store in the refrigerator for up to 1 week. The sauce can also be poured into an airtight container and frozen for up to 1 month.

6 **Warm or reheat the sauce, if needed**
To use refrigerated sauce at room temperature, remove the container from the refrigerator and let it stand for about 1 hour. Or, if the sauce is frozen, thaw it in the refrigerator for at least 6 hours, then let it stand at room temperature for about 1 hour. To reheat the sauce, place the desired quantity in a small saucepan over very low heat and warm, stirring often, until it is lukewarm, 3–4 minutes. Do not let it boil, which could burn the sauce.

**PASTRY CHEF'S TIP**
*If you use dark brown sugar and dark corn syrup, the sauce will have a deeper flavor. Using a mixture of light brown sugar and dark corn syrup is a good balance of flavors.*

# Sweetened Whipped Cream

Glossy, snow white, and billowy, whipped cream is a favorite addition to sundaes, parfaits, and other frozen desserts. Making it yourself is easy to do and yields delicious results. I like to infuse it with a hint of vanilla extract and just enough sugar to make it pleasingly sweet, but not cloying.

1 cup (8 fl oz/250 ml) cold heavy (double) cream

2 tablespoons confectioners' (icing) sugar

½ teaspoon vanilla extract (essence)

MAKES ABOUT 2 CUPS (16 FL OZ/500 ML)

### PASTRY CHEF'S TIP
*To whip heavy cream, use a large bowl. The larger the bowl, the easier it is to incorporate air. A deep bowl also prevents the cream from splattering.*

## 1 Ready the tools and equipment
Chilling the equipment before whipping will allow the cream to whip much faster and will also increase its stability. Place a deep, preferably metal mixing bowl (a metal bowl will stay colder than a plastic or glass bowl) and the whip attachment from a handheld mixer or stand mixer in the freezer until well chilled, at least 30 minutes.

## 2 Whip the cream to soft peaks
Pour the cold cream into the chilled bowl. (Cold cream whips faster and will achieve a greater volume than cream that is closer to room temperature.) Fit the mixer with the whip attachment. Turn on the mixer to low, and beat the cream until it is slightly thickened and little ridges are left on the surface of the cream when the whip is moved, about 1–2 minutes. Beating the cream on low speed at first prevents splattering, and the slow incorporation of air results in a more stable whipped cream. Increase the speed slowly to medium-high while continuing to beat, moving the whip around the bowl, if using a handheld mixer, so that the cream is evenly mixed. Beat just until the cream begins to hold a very soft (drooping) peak when you stop the mixer and lift the whip, 2–3 minutes.

## 3 Add the flavorings
The cream will achieve greater volume if the flavorings are added after it is whipped to soft peaks. Sprinkle the sugar over the softly whipped cream and add the vanilla. I like to use confectioners' sugar instead of granulated because its powdery consistency sweetens the cream without making it grainy.

4 **Whip the cream to firm peaks**
Continue to beat on medium-high speed until the cream holds firm peaks that stay upright with only a slight droop when the whip is lifted, 1–2 minutes more. Watch carefully to avoid overwhipping the cream, which will cause it to clump or look grainy. (If this happens, don't worry. To fix overwhipped cream, add 1–2 tablespoons unwhipped cream to loosen the mixture. Using a wire whisk, beat again just until firm peaks form.) In general, heavy cream should whip to about double its original volume.

5 **Use the whipped cream**
Use a large spoon to form dollops of whipped cream to top ice cream or other desserts. For a more decorative look, pipe the cream from a pastry bag. For more details on how to use a pastry bag, turn to page 39. Fit a pastry bag with a small fluted tip, secure it with the coupler, if needed, and fold down the top. Using a rubber spatula, scoop the whipped cream into the pastry bag filling it half full. Unfold the bag and twist the top, pressing the whipped cream toward the tip. Pipe the whipped cream in swirls on top of whatever you are garnishing.

6 **Store the whipped cream, if desired**
If possible, serve whipped cream immediately after whipping, when its volume and texture are at their best. You can also cover the mixing bowl with plastic wrap and store the cream in the refrigerator for up to 1 hour. If the mixture thins or becomes a bit watery while sitting, briefly beat with the mixer or a wire whisk to recombine and restore its volume.

**PASTRY CHEF'S TIP**
*An easy way to fill a pastry bag is to set the bag, tip down, into a tall cup or large liquid measuring cup. Fold down the top of the bag and then, using a rubber spatula, carefully fill the bag.*

# 2

# Key Techniques

Mastering the techniques in this chapter will make preparing

frozen desserts—and many other recipes—easier. In the

pages ahead, you will learn invaluable skills, from how to

separate eggs to how to caramelize sugar, that you will

use again and again when making the recipes in this book.

And you can always turn back to this chapter whenever

you need a refresher course.

# Separating Eggs

### 1 Crack the egg
Eggs are easiest to separate when cold. Have 3 clean, grease-free bowls ready. To reduce shell fragments, crack the side of the egg sharply on a flat surface, rather than the rim of a bowl.

### 2 Pull apart the shell halves
Hold the cracked egg over an empty bowl and carefully pull the shell apart, letting the white (but not the yolk) start to drop into the bowl.

### 3 Pass the yolk back and forth
Transfer the yolk back and forth from one shell half to the other, letting the white fall completely into the bowl below. Be careful not to break the yolk on a sharp shell edge.

### 4 Put the yolk in another bowl
Gently drop the yolk into the second bowl. Keeping the whites free of any yolk is key if you plan to whip the whites. A trace of yolk or other fat will prevent them from foaming.

**TROUBLESHOOTING**
If a yolk breaks as you separate the egg and gets into the white, this egg white cannot be used for whipping. Reserve the white for another use (like making scrambled eggs) or discard it. Rinse the bowl before continuing.

### 5 Put the white in another bowl
If the egg separates cleanly, pour the white into the third bowl. Break each new egg over the first empty bowl to avoid spoiling your batch of whites.

## Tempering Egg Yolks to Make Custard

### 1 Heat the milk mixture
Pour the milk mixture in a saucepan. Place over medium heat and cook, stirring with a wooden spoon, until bubbles form around the edges and the sugar is dissolved, 4–5 minutes.

### 2 Add cream to the egg yolks
Add cream to the mixing bowl holding the egg yolks. Whisk together until blended, 2–3 minutes. The cream will help insulate the yolks from the heat and prevent them from curdling.

### 3 Combine the mixtures
While whisking the egg-cream mixture, slowly pour one-fourth of the hot milk mixture into the bowl to gradually warm the yolks. This is known as *tempering* the yolks.

### 4 Heat the mixtures together
After one-fourth of the hot milk mixture has been blended into the yolks, pour the tempered yolk mixture back into the saucepan, whisking constantly until well blended.

**TROUBLESHOOTING**
Be sure to whisk the egg-cream mixture rapidly and constantly when pouring the hot milk mixture into it. If you don't, the custard could curdle. If this does happen, discard the mixture and start again with fresh ingredients.

### 5 Cook the custard
Cook until thick enough to coat a spoon, and drawing a finger along the spoon leaves a trail that does not fill in right away. It will register 160–170°F (71–77°C) on an instant-read thermometer.

## Chopping Chocolate

**1 Cut the chocolate into chunks**
Grasp the handle of a serrated or chef's knife with one hand and, with your other hand placed midpoint on the back of the blade, cut the chocolate into medium-sized pieces.

## Melting Chocolate

**1 Put the chocolate in a bowl**
Using a bench scraper, transfer the chopped chocolate to a metal bowl that fits on the rim of a saucepan. Add other ingredients, such as butter, if called for in the recipe.

**2 Set up a double boiler**
Pour water to a depth of about 1½ inches (4 cm) into the saucepan. Heat on low until it barely simmers. Place the bowl on top, making sure the bottom doesn't touch the water.

**2 Chop the chocolate into pieces**
Moving your other hand closer to the front of the blade, rock the knife to cut the chocolate into small, even pieces. The smaller and more uniform the pieces, the easier they will melt.

**3 Melt the chocolate**
Heat the chocolate, stirring often with a heatproof spatula, until melted and smooth, about 3–4 minutes. Using pot holders, lift out the bowl. Let the chocolate cool for 5 minutes.

**TROUBLESHOOTING**
Chocolate can *seize* when it comes into contact with moisture, such as water, during melting. To salvage it, remove it from the heat and stir in 1 tablespoon water at a time until the chocolate is smooth again.

## Chocolate Curls

**1 Run a peeler over the chocolate**
Soften the chocolate by holding
it in your hands for a minute or two.
Holding the chocolate with one hand,
use a vegetable peeler to scrape
curls 1½–2 inches (4–5 cm) long.

**2 Let the curls fall onto a pan**
Turn the chocolate block so that you
scrape from all sides, letting the
chocolate curls fall in a single layer
onto a rimmed baking sheet lined
with parchment (baking) paper.

## Grating Chocolate

**1 Grate the chocolate**
Holding a box grater-shredder with one
hand, quickly run a block of chocolate
over the shredding holes with the other.
Be sure the chocolate is cool to the
touch (it will melt easily).

**2 Place the gratings on a plate**
Let the gratings fall onto a work surface.
When you're ready to transfer them,
scoop them up with a bench scraper or
quickly pick them up with cool hands
as they will easily melt.

## Brewing Espresso

**1 Spoon the espresso into the filter**
A traditional Italian stove-top espresso
maker is economical and easy to use.
Fill the lower chamber with water and
then place the filter into the chamber
and fill with espresso grounds.

**2 Brew the espresso**
Screw the top onto the lower part of
the espresso maker. Place on the stove
top and bring to a boil. The water will
be forced up through the grounds to
make espresso.

## Caramelizing Sugar

### 1 Add the ingredients
Pour sugar, water, and lemon juice into a deep saucepan. The caramel will bubble up as it cooks, so make sure the pan is deep enough to keep it from bubbling over.

### 2 Add the corn syrup
Add the corn syrup to the ingredients in the saucepan. The corn syrup helps dissolve the sugar and will also prevent it from crystallizing.

### 3 Stir the mixture
Mix the ingredients together. They will look cloudy and grainy.

### 4 Cook the sugar
Place the saucepan over medium heat and stir constantly with a long-handled wooden spoon until no grains of sugar are visible, 1–2 minutes. Raise the heat to medium-high.

### 5 Check the color
As soon as you see the color turn a rich amber, or it registers 320–360°F (160–180°C) on a candy thermometer, about 2–4 minutes, immediately remove the pan from the heat.

**TROUBLESHOOTING**
You must watch the caramel vigilantly as it cooks, as it can turn dark within seconds. If the caramel looks very dark brown, it is burnt and will have an unpleasant flavor. The lighter the color, the more mild the flavor will be.

## Working with a Vanilla Bean

**1 Split the bean lengthwise**
Using a paring knife, hold the pod in place and carefully cut down the center lengthwise.

**2 Scrape out the seeds**
Using the tip of the knife, scrape the seeds from the inside of each pod half. The seeds will stick, so you may need to scrape twice.

## Filling a Pastry Bag

**1 Fit the tip into the bag**
Fit a decorating tip in the hole of a pastry bag. Depending on the bag's manufacturer, you may need to use a small, white device called a *coupler* to hold it in place.

**2 Fill the bag**
Fold down the top of the bag to form a cuff that is one-third the length of the bag. Place one hand under the cuff. Using a rubber spatula, scoop the mixture into the bag, filling it half full.

**TROUBLESHOOTING**
If you don't have a coupler, twist the empty bag near the tip and then push the bag down into the tip. This will create a barrier and ensure that nothing will leak out while you fill the bag.

**3 Twist the tip of the bag**
To ensure against air bubbles, and to keep the mixture flowing well, twist the bag several times at the point where the mixture ends.

## TECHNIQUE · Working with Mint

### 1 Roll up the leaves
After rinsing the mint leaves, dry them well (wet leaves will stick to the knife). Stack the leaves and roll the stack lengthwise into a cylinder. Try to roll the leaves as tightly as possible.

### 2 Cut the leaves
Using a chef's knife, cut the leaves crosswise into narrow ribbons. These ribbons are known as *chiffonade*.

## TECHNIQUE · Zesting & Juicing Citrus

### 1 Zest the lemon
Wash the fruit well. Use a rasp grater, such as a Microplane grater, or the finest rasps on a box grater-shredder to remove the colored part of the peel, not the bitter white pith.

### 2 Clean off the grater
Don't forget to scrape all the zest from the back of the grater, where some of it naturally gathers.

### 3 Cut the lemon in half
To juice a lemon, first press and roll it firmly against the counter to break some of the membranes holding in the juice. Then, using a chef's knife, cut the fruit in half crosswise.

### 4 Juice the lemon
To extract as much juice as possible, use a citrus reamer to pierce the membranes as you squeeze. Catch the juice in a bowl, and strain to remove seeds before using.

# Working with Melon

### 1 Cut the melon in half
Place the melon on its side on a flat surface. Put a hand on one end of the melon to secure it in place. Using a chef's knife, carefully but firmly cut the melon in half crosswise.

### 2 Scoop out the seeds
Use a large spoon to scoop out the seeds from the center of the melon and discard the seeds. Sometimes it is helpful to tilt the melon slightly to make it more stable.

### 3 Cut the melon halves into wedges
Stand a melon half hollow side up. Using a chef's knife, cut in half. Repeat with the other melon half. You should have a total of 4 wedges.

### 4 Remove the flesh from the skin
One at a time, stand each wedge, skin side down, on the surface. Carefully cut the flesh from the skin, following the contour of the wedge.

### 5 Cut the wedges into portions
Lay each wedge on a flat surface. Cut each wedge lengthwise into even semicircular portions.

### 6 Cut the portions into rough cubes
Working with 1 or 2 melon portions at a time, cut crosswise into rough cube-shaped pieces.

## Peeling Peaches

### 1 Score the bottom

The best way to peel peaches and other thin-skinned fruits is to plunge them into boiling water, or *blanch* them. First, use a paring knife to cut a shallow X on the bottom.

### 2 Place in boiling water

Fill a large saucepan three-fourths full of water and bring to a boil. Using a slotted spoon, lower 1 or 2 peaches in the water. Let them sit until the skin loosens, 15–30 seconds.

## Scooping Ice Cream, Gelato & Sorbet

### 1 Warm the scoop

Place the scoop in a measuring cup or bowl filled with hot water for 10 seconds, until the scoop is warm.

### 3 Transfer to ice water

Immediately transfer the peach(es) to a bowl three-fourths full of ice water. This step, called *shocking*, will stop the cooking process.

### 4 Peel the skin

When the fruit is cool enough to handle, find the X you made in step 1. Grasp a corner of loose skin between your thumb and a paring knife and pull off the skin. Repeat to peel fully.

### 2 Form the ice cream into a scoop

Remove the scoop from the water and let dry briefly. Push the scoop into the ice cream, gelato, or sorbet and move it from one side to the other to form a rounded scoop.

# Slicing Frozen Tortes

## 1 Mark the center

A torte is easiest to cut if solidly frozen, so be sure that it has been in the freezer for at least 3 hours. Lightly insert a toothpick or round wooden skewer into the center of the cake.

## 2 Mark the slices

Starting at the center, and with the toothpick as a guide, use a chef's knife to score the slices gently. Cut down lightly on each mark, but don't cut all the way through the cake.

## 3 Warm the knife

Have ready a tall pitcher filled with very hot tap water. Before each cut, place the chef's knife in the water to warm it, which will ease slicing through the frozen layers.

## 4 Wipe the knife clean

Use a clean paper towel to dry off and clean the knife after each cut. Hold the sharp side of the knife away from you and wipe from the dull side.

## 5 Cut the torte

Using the warm, clean chef's knife, cut the torte into individual slices. The knife should easily cut through the cold ingredients.

## 6 Serve the slices

Use a triangular cake server to lift up each slice and place it on a plate. The first slice may not be as pretty as the rest, so reserve that piece for yourself.

# 3

# Ice Cream
# & Gelato

Nothing you can buy can compare to homemade ice cream and gelato. Once you understand how simple it is to make a custard base and churn it to create smooth, creamy ice cream or gelato, you will always want to make your own. The classic ice cream flavors—vanilla, chocolate, and strawberry—are all included here, but you will also find more than a dozen others, plus two gelatos and a sherbet.

# French Vanilla Ice Cream

The hallmarks of this French-style ice cream are a lush, satiny texture and a full flavor, products of churning a carefully cooked custard base of eggs, milk, and cream. The pod and the seeds of a vanilla bean impart a unique floral aroma, while the seeds add a scattering of dark speckles to the finished ice cream.

## 1 Separate the eggs

If you need help separating eggs, turn to page 34. Have ready 2 small bowls and 1 larger heatproof glass or stainless-steel bowl. Holding an egg in your hand, strike it sharply on its equator on the work surface, cracking it, then hold it upright over 1 small bowl and lift away the top half of the shell. The yolk should be resting in the bottom half. Working gently so as not to break the yolk, transfer the yolk back and forth between the shell halves over the bowl, allowing all the egg white to drop into the bowl. Drop the yolk into the heatproof bowl and transfer the white to the other small bowl. Repeat with the remaining 5 eggs. Set the yolks aside. Reserve the whites for another use, such as making meringue for Individual Baked Alaskas (page 113).

## 2 Split the vanilla bean

Using a paring knife, carefully slit the vanilla bean down the center lengthwise. You may not be able to do this in a single stroke, as the vanilla bean can be awkward to work with, but cutting in stages is fine. You will notice a dark brown, pasty substance on the inside of each pod half. This is actually hundreds of tiny vanilla seeds. Use the tip of the knife to scrape the seeds from the bean and add them to a medium saucepan. You may need to do the scraping twice, as the seeds tend to stick to the vanilla bean pod. Also, the seeds will stick to the knife, so make sure you get them all into the pan. Add the vanilla bean pod to the saucepan as well (most of the flavor comes from here). For more details on how to split a vanilla bean, turn to page 39.

## 3 Prepare the custard ingredients

Add the milk, 1 cup (8 fl oz/250 ml) of the cream, and the sugar to the saucepan with the vanilla bean. Add the remaining ½ cup (4 fl oz/125 ml) cream to the bowl with the egg yolks. Using a whisk, mix the yolks and cream together vigorously until they are blended and a pale buttery yellow, 2–3 minutes. >

6 large eggs

1 large, soft vanilla bean

1½ cups (12 fl oz/375 ml) whole milk

1½ cups (12 fl oz/375 ml) heavy (double) cream

¾ cup (6 oz/185 g) granulated sugar

MAKES ABOUT 1 QUART (1 LITER)

**PASTRY CHEF'S TIP**
*If your vanilla bean has been exposed to air and has hardened, place it in a jar and add milk to cover completely. Refrigerate for 2 days, then rinse with water and use. The bean should be soft.*

## 4 Temper the egg yolks

Place the saucepan over medium heat and cook, stirring frequently with a wooden spoon, until bubbles form around the edges, the liquid just begins to ripple in the center, and the sugar is dissolved, 4–5 minutes. Do not allow to come to a boil because the liquid will boil up and over the edges of the saucepan very quickly. Remove the pan from the heat. Begin whisking the egg yolk mixture with one hand while slowly pouring one-fourth of the hot milk mixture into the yolks with the other. This method of slowly adding hot liquid to egg yolks is called *tempering*. When one-fourth of the hot milk mixture has been blended into the yolks, pour the warmed yolk mixture back into the saucepan, whisking constantly until well blended. To find out more about tempering eggs, turn to page 35.

## 5 Cook and strain the custard

Place the saucepan with the milk-and-yolk mixture over medium heat and cook, stirring constantly with a wooden spoon, for 4–5 minutes. Make sure you reach all areas on the bottom of the saucepan to ensure that the custard does not scorch or curdle. The custard should come to a bare simmer, with steam rising from the surface and the surface rippling, but it should not reach a boil. It is ready when it is thick enough to coat the back of the spoon, and if you draw your finger along the spoon, it leaves a trail that does not fill in immediately. Remove from the heat. Set a fine mesh sieve over a bowl. Pour the hot custard through the sieve, pressing the liquid through with the back of the spoon and leaving any grainy solids in the sieve along with the vanilla bean pod. Discard the pod or reuse.

## 6 Cool the custard

Fill a large mixing bowl halfway with ice cubes and enough water just to cover the ice cubes. Place the bowl with the custard into the larger bowl, nestling the medium bowl into the ice cubes. Let the custard cool, stirring occasionally, until it reaches room temperature, 30–45 minutes. Once the custard has cooled to room temperature, remove the medium bowl from the ice-water bath. >

### PASTRY CHEF'S TIP

*Used vanilla bean pods can be saved to flavor sugar. Rinse in water, dry with a paper towel, and bury deep in a sugar canister. Use the sugar to flavor freshly whipped cream, or coffee, or to decorate sugar cookies.*

### 7 Chill the custard

Place a piece of plastic wrap directly on the surface of the custard, which will prevent a coating, or "skin," from forming. Cover the top of the bowl with plastic wrap and refrigerate until the custard is well chilled, at least 3 hours or up to 24 hours. A well-chilled custard will freeze more effectively and have a better flavor.

### 8 Churn the ice cream

Prepare an ice cream maker with at least a 1-quart (1-l) capacity according to the manufacturer's directions. Remove the plastic wrap from the custard and bowl. Pour the well-chilled custard into the mixing container of the ice cream maker and churn according to the manufacturer's directions until the custard reaches the consistency of thick whipped cream. The timing will depend on the type of machine you are using and the temperature of the custard.

### PASTRY CHEF'S TIP

*If you don't have a vanilla bean, you can substitute pure vanilla extract (essence) in most recipes; never use imitation vanilla, which has an inferior flavor. Use 1½ teaspoons extract for each vanilla bean. Because vanilla extract is alcohol based and will evaporate when heated, add it to the custard just as it finishes cooking.*

### 9 Store the ice cream

The ice cream can be served immediately, directly from the mixing container, but it will have a very soft consistency and a mild flavor. For a fuller flavor and a firmer consistency more like that of traditional ice cream, use a rubber spatula to transfer the ice cream to a plastic freezer container. Cover tightly and freeze until the ice cream is firm, at least 3 hours or up to 3 days. It is best served 6 to 12 hours after being transferred to the freezer.

### 10 Serve the ice cream

To serve the ice cream, dip an ice cream scoop into hot water and warm briefly. Pull the scoop across the ice cream to form a rounded scoop. For more details on how to scoop ice cream, turn to page 42. Store any remaining ice cream, tightly covered, in the freezer.

## Serving Ideas

*Vanilla ice cream has a mellow flavor that pairs well with other elements. You can combine it with a full-flavored chocolate sorbet and top with grated chocolate or white chocolate curls, or you can coat small scoops with crushed tuile cookies to make delicious bonbons. And vanilla ice cream dressed up with butterscotch sauce, sliced almonds, and whipped cream is an irresistible sundae any day of the week.*

**Black-and-white sundae** (top left)
Pair scoops of creamy vanilla ice cream with intense Chocolate Sorbet (page 88) in a martini glass. Top with white chocolate curls (page 37) for a sophisticated dessert.

**Ice cream bonbons** (left)
Place small scoops of vanilla ice cream on a baking sheet lined with waxed paper and put in the freezer for 10 minutes. Remove from the freezer and roll the scoops in finely crushed Tuile Cookies (page 22).

**Butterscotch sundae** (above)
Pair scoops of ice cream with Butterscotch Sauce (page 28), Sweetened Whipped Cream (page 30), and sliced (flaked) almonds.

# French-Style Ice Cream Variations

The custard base—a slowly cooked mixture of milk, cream, sugar, and tempered egg yolks—that you learned to make for French Vanilla Ice Cream (page 47) is the first step to making many popular ice cream flavors, including the six ideas that appear here. For some of them, you add flavorings—including ground dark-roast coffee, cinnamon, coconut, or caramelized sugar—to the custard as it cooks; in another, you replace part of the cream with ultrarich mascarpone cheese. And in still another, you layer the vanilla ice cream with thick chocolate sauce and then freeze the mixture to create chocolate-swirled vanilla. Each variation makes 1 quart (1 l) ice cream.

### Espresso Ice Cream

Give this ice cream an extra jolt of flavor by pouring a spoonful or two of Kahlúa over each serving. You can also add ½ cup (½ oz/15 g) chopped chocolate-covered coffee beans during the last 5 minutes of churning.

Follow the recipe to make French Vanilla Ice Cream. When adding the vanilla seeds and vanilla bean pod to the saucepan in step 2, stir in ¼ cup (½ oz/15 g) coarsely ground espresso.

Proceed with the recipe to make the custard and churn the ice cream.

Scoop the ice cream and serve.

### Cinnamon Ice Cream

A cinnamon stick results in a mild cinnamon flavor, while ground cinnamon imparts a more potent flavor and dots the ice cream with rust-colored speckles.

Follow the recipe to make French Vanilla Ice Cream. When adding the vanilla seeds and vanilla bean pod to the saucepan in step 2, stir in one 3-inch (7.5-cm) cinnamon stick or ½ teaspoon ground cinnamon.

Proceed with the recipe to make the custard and churn the ice cream (be sure to remove the cinnamon stick before you begin churning).

Scoop the ice cream and serve.

### Vanilla-Chocolate Swirl Ice Cream

Vanilla and chocolate are America's favorite ice cream flavors, so swirling the two together will appeal to nearly everyone.

Make 1 batch French Vanilla Ice Cream (page 47). Next, make 1 batch Chocolate Sauce (page 24) and let cool to room temperature.

Using an offset spatula, layer about one-fifth of the ice cream in a deep 1½-quart (1.5-l) freezerproof container. Using an offset spatula, spread ¼–⅓ cup (2–3 fl oz/60–80 ml) of the sauce on top of the ice cream. Repeat the layering process to use all of the ice cream and one-half to three-fourths of the chocolate sauce, ending with a layer of ice cream. Save the remaining sauce for another use. Cover tightly and freeze for at least 3 hours or up to 3 days.

To serve, scoop down through several layers to form the swirls.

## Coconut Ice Cream

This ice cream is especially delicious with warm Chocolate Sauce (page 24) or with grilled pineapple slices.

In a small saucepan, whisk together 1 cup (8 fl oz/250 ml) whole milk, ½ cup (4 fl oz/125 ml) unsweetened coconut milk, 1 cup (8 fl oz/250 ml) heavy (double) cream, and ⅔ cup (5 oz/155 g) granulated sugar. Stir in ½ cup (2 oz/60 g) sweetened or unsweetened flaked dried coconut and the seeds from 1 vanilla bean. Warm over medium heat, stirring often, until the sugar dissolves and small bubbles form around the edges, 4–5 minutes. Remove from the heat and let stand for 10 minutes. Strain through a fine-mesh sieve into a clean saucepan to remove all the flaked coconut. Press on the coconut to extract as much liquid as possible.

Warm the coconut-milk mixture over medium heat until bubbles form around the edges. In a small bowl, whisk together 6 large egg yolks and ½ cup (4 fl oz/125 ml) heavy (double) cream until blended. Whisk one-fourth of the coconut-milk mixture into the yolks. Then whisk the yolk mixture back into the saucepan with the remaining coconut-milk mixture. Heat over medium-low heat, stirring constantly, until thickened, 4–5 minutes. Stir in 3 tablespoons cream of coconut.

Proceed with the recipe starting at step 6 to cool the custard, then churn and serve the ice cream.

## Caramel Ice Cream

Serve this ice cream plain or topped with Chocolate Sauce (page 24) or Caramel Sauce (page 26).

In a deep, 2-qt (2-l) saucepan, combine ¾ cup (6 oz/185 g) granulated sugar, 2 tablespoons water, 2 teaspoons light corn syrup, and ½ teaspoon fresh lemon juice. Warm over medium heat, stirring until the sugar dissolves and the liquid is clear and bubbling, 1–2 minutes. Raise the heat to medium-high and boil gently, stirring occasionally, until the mixture is a rich amber. Remove from the heat and slowly pour ¾ cup (6 fl oz/180 ml) heavy (double) cream into the caramel, stirring until smooth. If it isn't smooth, return to low heat and stir again until smooth. Let cool to room temperature.

In a small saucepan, stir together 1½ cups (12 fl oz/375 ml) whole milk and ¾ cup (6 fl oz/180 ml) heavy (double) cream. Stir in the caramel mixture. Warm over medium heat, stirring often, until small bubbles form around the edges. Remove from the heat.

In a small bowl, whisk together 6 large egg yolks and ½ cup (4 fl oz/125 ml) heavy (double) cream until blended. Whisk one-fourth of the caramel-milk mixture into the yolks. Then whisk the yolk mixture back into the saucepan with the remaining caramel-milk mixture. Heat over medium-low heat, stirring constantly, until thickened, 4–5 minutes.

Proceed with the recipe starting at step 6 to cool the custard, then churn and serve the ice cream.

## Mascarpone Ice Cream

When mascarpone is substituted for part of the heavy cream, the resulting ice cream is an intensely creamy dessert that resembles a semifrozen cheesecake.

In a small saucepan, whisk together 1½ cups (12 fl oz/375 ml) whole milk, 1 cup (8 fl oz/250 ml) heavy (double) cream, and ¾ cup (6 oz/185 g) granulated sugar. Stir in the seeds from 1 vanilla bean. Warm over medium heat, stirring often, until the sugar dissolves and small bubbles form around the edges. Remove from the heat.

In a small bowl, whisk together 4 large egg yolks and ½ cup (4 fl oz/125 ml) heavy (double) cream until blended. Whisk one-fourth of the milk mixture into the yolks to warm them. Then whisk the yolk mixture back into the saucepan with the remaining milk mixture. Heat over medium-low heat, stirring constantly, until thickened, 4–5 minutes.

Strain the custard, then gently whisk in ½ teaspoon almond extract (essence) and ½ cup (4 oz/125 g) room-temperature mascarpone until the mascarpone is melted and the custard is smooth.

Proceed with the recipe starting at step 6 to cool the custard, then churn and serve the ice cream.

# Strawberry Ice Cream

The secret to making the best strawberry ice cream is to start with the juiciest, ripest, and most flavorful fruits. When added to the rich custard base during the last few minutes of churning, the chopped berries retain their texture and intensely fruity flavor and punctuate the pale pink ice cream with bright flecks.

1 c. ← 2 cups (8 oz/250 g) stemmed and coarsely chopped strawberries

¼ c. ← ½ cup (4 oz/125 g) plus 2 tablespoons granulated sugar

½ c. ← 1 cup (8 fl oz/250 ml) whole milk

½ c. ← 1 cup (8 fl oz/250 ml) heavy (double) cream

1½ yolk ← 3 large egg yolks (page 34)

¼ 1 teaspoon vanilla extract (essence)

MAKES ABOUT 1 QUART (1 LITER)

**PASTRY CHEF'S TIP**

*If you want to make Strawberry Ice Cream when strawberries are out of season in your area, use high-quality frozen berries, rather than out-of-season berries shipped in from long distances. Frozen fruit is often picked at peak ripeness and quick-frozen within a few hours. Use 2 cups (8–10 oz/250–315 g) unsweetened or lightly sweetened frozen sliced or whole berries.*

**1 Purée the strawberries**
Put half of the chopped strawberries in a food processor along with 2 tablespoons of the sugar. Purée the strawberries until smooth, stopping once or twice to scrape down the sides of the bowl with a rubber spatula. Set aside the puréed berries and remaining chopped berries in separate small bowls.

**2 Prepare the custard ingredients**
Put the milk, ¾ cup (6 fl oz/180 ml) of the cream, and the remaining ½ cup sugar in a medium saucepan. In a small bowl, whisk together the egg yolks and the remaining ¼ cup (2 fl oz/60 ml) cream until they are blended and a pale buttery yellow, about 1 minute.

**3 Temper the egg yolks**
Place the saucepan over medium heat and cook, stirring frequently with a wooden spoon, until bubbles form around the edges, the liquid just begins to ripple in the center, and the sugar is dissolved, 4–5 minutes. Do not allow the liquid to come to a boil. Remove from the heat. Begin whisking the egg yolk mixture with one hand while slowly pouring one-fourth of the hot milk mixture into the yolks with the other. This method of slowly adding a hot liquid to egg yolks is called *tempering*. When one-fourth of the hot milk mixture has been blended into the yolks, start pouring the warmed yolk mixture back into the saucepan, whisking constantly until well blended. To find out more about tempering eggs, turn to page 35.

**4 Cook the custard**
Place the saucepan with the milk-and-yolk mixture over medium heat, stirring constantly with a wooden spoon, 4–5 minutes. It should be thick enough to coat the back of a spoon. While the custard cooks it is important to stir it constantly, taking care to reach all areas on the bottom of the saucepan so that it does not scorch or curdle. The custard should come to a bare simmer, with steam rising from the surface and the surface rippling, but it should not actually bubble or come to a boil.

**5 Add the pureed fruit and strain the custard**
Remove the saucepan from the heat and stir in the puréed strawberries and vanilla extract. Set a fine-mesh sieve over a medium bowl. Pour the hot custard through the sieve, gently pressing the liquid through with the back of the spoon and leaving any grainy solids and strawberry seeds in the sieve. ›

### 6 Cool the custard

Fill a large mixing bowl halfway with ice cubes and enough cold water just to cover the ice cubes. Place the bowl with the custard into the larger bowl, nestling the medium bowl into the ice cubes. Let the custard cool, stirring occasionally, until it reaches room temperature, 30–45 minutes. As the ice melts, be sure the water level does not rise to flood into the custard. Once the custard has cooled to room temperature, remove the medium bowl from the ice water bath.

### 7 Chill the custard

Place a piece of plastic wrap directly onto the surface of the custard, which will prevent a coating, or "skin," from forming as the custard chills. Cover the top of the bowl with plastic wrap and refrigerate the custard until it is well chilled, at least 3 hours or up to 12 hours.

### 8 Churn the ice cream and add the fruit

Prepare an ice cream maker with at least a 1-quart (1-l) capacity according to the manufacturer's directions. Remove the plastic wrap from the custard and bowl. Pour the well-chilled custard into the mixing container of the ice cream maker and freeze according to the manufacturer's directions. The timing will depend on the type of machine and the temperature of the custard. During the last few minutes of churning, when the custard has reached the consistency of thick whipped cream, add the reserved 1 cup (4 oz/125 g) coarsely chopped strawberries and churn just until incorporated. Unlike fruit ice cream purchased at the supermarket, which may have bright coloring added, homemade strawberry ice cream will be a very pale pink, with flecks of berries in it.

### 9 Store the ice cream

The ice cream can be served immediately, directly from the mixing container, but it will have a very soft consistency and a mild flavor. For a fuller flavor and a firmer consistency more like that of traditional ice cream, use a rubber spatula to transfer the ice cream to a plastic freezer container. Cover tightly and freeze until the ice cream is firm, at least 3 hours or up to 2 days. It is best served 3 to 6 hours after being transferred to the freezer.

### 10 Serve the ice cream

To serve the ice cream, dip an ice cream scoop into hot water and warm briefly. Pull the scoop across the ice cream to form a rounded scoop. For more details on how to scoop ice cream, turn to page 42. Store any remaining ice cream, tightly covered, in the freezer.

# Fruit Ice Cream Variations

Now that you have learned how to add fruit to the custard base of a French-style ice cream to make Strawberry Ice Cream (page 54), you can substitute other fruits for the strawberries. In every case, use the best fruit available. This means either choosing fresh fruit, preferably locally grown and in its natural season, or using the best-quality frozen fruit you can find. Raspberries, peaches, and bananas are popular choices, but blackberries, cherries, and nectarines are equally good. Watery fruits such as melons and acidic fruits such as grapefruit are best reserved for making granitas (pages 91–97). Each variation makes 1 quart (1 l).

## Raspberry Ice Cream

If berries are not in season, or you can't find flavorful, fresh local berries, frozen berries are a good substitute.

Follow the recipe for Strawberry Ice Cream, substituting **2 cups (8 oz/250 g) whole fresh or thawed, frozen raspberries** for the strawberries. To intensify the raspberry flavor, add **1 tablespoon framboise or other raspberry liqueur** along with the vanilla extract in step 5.

Proceed with the recipe to make the custard and churn the ice cream.

## Peach Ice Cream

Look for tree-ripened peaches, which have more flavor than peaches picked when immature. They will be a bit more expensive, but the flavor is worth it.

Follow the recipe for Strawberry Ice Cream, substituting **2 cups (8 oz/250 g) peeled and coarsely chopped peaches (about 2 large peaches)** tossed with **2 teaspoons fresh lemon juice** for the strawberries. If desired, add **1 tablespoon dark rum, sherry, or brandy** along with the vanilla extract in step 5.

Proceed with the recipe to make the custard and churn the ice cream.

**PASTRY CHEF'S TIP**
*If you don't plan to use peeled peaches right away, toss them with 1–2 teaspoons of fresh lemon juice to keep the flesh from discoloring when exposed to the air.*

## Banana Ice Cream

Buy bananas that are firm and yellow, with only slight tinges of green, then let them ripen on a countertop until they are completely yellow, are slightly soft when gently pressed, and have a few brown spots evenly spaced all over the fruit.

Follow the recipe for Strawberry Ice Cream, substituting **1½ cups (9 oz/290 g) peeled, sliced bananas (about 2 medium bananas)** tossed with **1 tablespoon fresh lemon juice** for the strawberries.

Proceed with the recipe to make the custard and churn the ice cream.

To complement or intensify the banana flavor, add **1 tablespoon dark rum or banana liqueur** when the ice cream is nearly finished churning and is the consistency of thick whipped cream.

# Chocolate Ice Cream

In this recipe, both dark chocolate and intensely flavored cocoa powder are added to a custard base to create the signature brown color and rich flavor of this wildly popular ice cream. Vanilla extract contributes flavor and also softens the natural bitterness of the dark chocolate and cocoa powder.

## 1 Chop the chocolate

If you need help chopping chocolate, turn to page 36. Place the chocolate on a cutting board. Use a serrated knife or chef's knife to cut the chocolate into large chunks. (You don't want to touch the chocolate with your hand, as it could cause the chocolate to melt prematurely.) Then, using a rocking motion, cut the chocolate into even pieces. Be sure the pieces are small so that they will melt quickly. Put the chopped chocolate in a small heatproof bowl.

## 2 Prepare the custard ingredients

Put the milk, 1 cup (8 fl oz/250 ml) of the cream, and the sugar in a medium saucepan. In a small bowl, whisk together the egg yolks and the remaining ½ cup (4 fl oz/125 ml) cream until they are blended and a pale buttery yellow, about 1 minute. Sprinkle the cocoa powder over the yolk mixture and whisk until evenly colored and no lumps remain, about 1–2 minutes.

## 3 Temper the egg yolks

Place the saucepan over medium heat and cook, stirring frequently with a wooden spoon, until bubbles form around the edges, the liquid just begins to ripple in the center, and the sugar is dissolved, 4–5 minutes. Do not allow the liquid to come to a boil. Remove from the heat. Begin whisking the egg yolk mixture with one hand while slowly pouring one-fourth of the hot milk mixture into the yolks with the other. This method of slowly adding a hot liquid to egg yolks is called *tempering*. When one-fourth of the hot milk mixture has been blended into the yolks, start pouring the warmed yolk mixture back into the saucepan, whisking constantly until well blended. To find out more about tempering eggs, turn to page 35.

## 4 Cook the custard

Place the saucepan with the milk-and-yolk mixture over medium heat, stirring constantly with a wooden spoon, 4–5 minutes. It should be thick enough to coat the back of a spoon. While the custard cooks it is important to stir it constantly, taking care to reach all areas on the bottom of the saucepan so that it does not scorch or curdle. The custard should come to a bare simmer, with steam rising from the surface and the surface rippling, but it should not actually bubble or come to a boil. >

6 oz (185 g) bittersweet or semisweet (plain) chocolate, broken into pieces

1½ cups (12 fl oz/375 ml) whole milk

1½ cups (12 fl oz/375 ml) heavy (double) cream

⅔ cup (5 oz/155 g) granulated sugar

4 large egg yolks (page 34)

3 tablespoons unsweetened regular or Dutch-process cocoa powder

2 teaspoons vanilla extract (essence)

MAKES ABOUT 1 QUART (1 L)

**PASTRY CHEF'S TIP**
*If your solid chocolate looks pale, powdery, or blotchy, it has bloomed, a result of storing it where it was too warm or too humid. The chocolate can still be used for making ice cream, although the flavor may be less intense.*

### 5 Add the chocolate and vanilla extract

Remove the saucepan from the heat. Sprinkle the chopped chocolate over the top of the custard and let stand for 1 minute so that the chocolate begins to melt. Then, using a wooden spoon, stir gently until the chocolate is melted and the custard is smooth, about 2 minutes. Stir in the vanilla extract until blended.

### 6 Strain and chill the custard

Set a fine-mesh sieve over a medium bowl. Pour the hot custard through the sieve, gently pressing the liquid through with the back of the spoon and leaving any grainy solids in the sieve. Fill a large mixing bowl halfway with ice cubes and enough cold water just to cover the ice cubes. Place the bowl with the custard into the larger bowl and let cool for 30–45 minutes. Once the custard has cooled to room temperature, remove the medium bowl from the ice water bath. Place a piece of plastic wrap directly onto the surface of the custard, which will prevent a coating, or "skin," from forming as the custard chills. Cover the top of the bowl with plastic wrap and refrigerate the custard until it is well chilled, at least 3 hours or up to 24 hours.

### 7 Churn the ice cream

Prepare an ice cream maker with at least a 1-quart (1-l) capacity according to the manufacturer's directions. Remove the plastic wrap from the custard and bowl. Pour the well-chilled custard into the mixing container of the ice cream maker and freeze according to the manufacturer's directions. The timing will depend on the type of machine and the temperature of the custard.

### 8 Store the ice cream

The ice cream can be served immediately, directly from the mixing container, but it will have a very soft consistency and a mild flavor. For fuller flavor and a firmer consistency more like that of traditional ice cream, use a rubber spatula to transfer the ice cream to a plastic freezer container. Cover tightly and freeze until the ice cream is firm, at least 3 hours or up to 3 days. It is best served 6 to 12 hours after being transferred to the freezer.

### 9 Serve the ice cream

To serve the ice cream, dip an ice cream scoop into hot water and warm briefly. Pull the scoop across the ice cream to form a rounded scoop. For more details on how to scoop ice cream, turn to page 42. Store any remaining ice cream, tightly covered, in the freezer.

# Chocolate Ice Cream Variations

The cocoa butter in dark chocolate gives the Chocolate Ice Cream on page 59 a particularly rich quality, so any additions to the recipe are gilding the lily. But chocolate lovers often like to do just that, and once you are confident making the basic ice cream, you can turn to these variations to create three more flavors. The addition of amaretto results in a sophisticated adult dessert, while the other two variations, one laced with bits of chocolate and the other with nuts and marshmallows, are appreciated by all ages. As always, buy the best ingredients that you can afford. Each variation makes 1 quart (1 l).

## Chocolate-Amaretto Ice Cream

Amaretto is alcohol based, so this ice cream will not freeze as firmly as chocolate ice cream made without it.

Follow the recipe for Chocolate Ice Cream. During the last 1–2 minutes of churning in step 7, when the ice cream is the consistency of thick whipped cream, add 3 tablespoons amaretto liqueur and continue to churn until blended.

Proceed with the recipe to store and serve the ice cream.

## Chocolate–Chocolate Chip Ice Cream

For this recipe, I like to use either finely chopped bittersweet or semisweet (plain) chocolate or miniature chocolate chips.

Follow the recipe for Chocolate Ice Cream. During the last 1–2 minutes of churning in step 7, when the ice cream is the consistency of thick whipped cream, add 1 cup (6 oz/185 g) finely chopped bittersweet or semisweet (plain) chocolate or miniature chocolate chips and continue to churn until blended.

Proceed with the recipe to store and serve the ice cream.

## Rocky Road Ice Cream

Here, walnuts and miniature marshmallows are added to the ice cream just before it has finished churning to make an old-fashioned favorite.

Follow the recipe for Chocolate Ice Cream. During the last 1–2 minutes of churning in step 7, when the ice cream is the consistency of thick whipped cream, add ⅓ cup (1½ oz/45 g) chopped walnuts and ⅓ cup (½ oz/15 g) miniature marshmallows and continue to churn until blended.

Proceed with the recipe to store and serve the ice cream.

**PASTRY CHEF'S TIP**

*The addition of any solid ingredient to ice cream that is being churned in an electric machine can cause the paddle to jam. Add chocolate chips, nuts, marshmallows, or similar items during the last minute or two, and churn just long enough to incorporate. Watch the machine closely during this time; if the paddle jams, you may need to stir in the ingredients by hand.*

# Mint–Chocolate Chip Ice Cream

Fresh mint and high-quality chocolate give this ice cream an extraordinary flavor. The potency of the mint leaves and the length of time that they are left in the milk will determine the depth of the mint flavor. The ice cream will be a pale green, rather than the artificially created neon green of many commercial mint ice creams.

1½ cups (12 fl oz/375 ml) whole milk

1½ cups (12 fl oz/375 ml) heavy (double) cream

⅔ cup (5 oz/150 g) granulated sugar

1 cup (1 oz/30 g) fresh mint leaves, from about 1 bunch

4 large egg yolks (page 34)

½ teaspoon vanilla extract (essence)

4 oz (125 g) bittersweet or semisweet (plain) chocolate, coarsely chopped (page 36), melted (page 36), and cooled to room temperature

2 teaspoons canola oil

MAKES ABOUT 1 QUART (1 L)

**PASTRY CHEF'S TIP**

*For a deeper green and a more minty flavor, add 2 tablespoons green crème de menthe while the ice cream is churning. If you have only white crème de menthe, it can be added for flavor only.*

1 **Prepare the custard ingredients**
Put the milk, 1 cup (8 fl oz/250 ml) of the cream, ⅓ cup (2½ oz/75 g) of the sugar, and the mint leaves in a medium saucepan. Place the saucepan over medium heat and cook, stirring frequently with a wooden spoon, until bubbles form around the edges, the liquid begins to ripple in the center, and the sugar is dissolved, 4–5 minutes. Remove from the heat and let it stand for 15–20 minutes. In a medium bowl, whisk together the egg yolks, the remaining ⅓ cup sugar, and the remaining ½ cup (4 fl oz/125 ml) cream until blended.

2 **Temper the egg yolks and cook the custard**
To find out more about tempering eggs, turn to page 35. Return the saucepan to medium heat and cook, stirring frequently until bubbles again form around the edges, 2–4 minutes. Remove from the heat. Begin whisking the egg yolk mixture while slowly pouring one-fourth of the hot milk mixture into the yolks. Then slowly pour the warmed yolk mixture back into the saucepan, whisking constantly until well blended. Place the saucepan back over medium heat and stir constantly until the mixture has thickened, 4–5 minutes.

3 **Strain and chill the custard**
Set a fine-mesh sieve over a medium bowl. Pour the hot custard through the sieve, pressing on the mint to release as much liquid as possible. Discard the mint leaves. Stir in the vanilla extract. Fill a large mixing bowl halfway with ice cubes and enough cold water just to cover the ice cubes. Place the bowl with the custard into the larger bowl and let cool for 30–45 minutes. Remove the bowl with the custard and place a piece of plastic wrap directly onto the surface of the custard and on top of the bowl. Refrigerate for 3 hours or up to 24 hours.

4 **Churn the ice cream and add the chocolate**
Prepare an ice cream maker with at least a 1-quart (1-l) capacity according to the manufacturer's directions. Remove the plastic wrap from the custard and bowl, pour into the ice cream maker, and churn. About 1–2 minutes before the end of churning, drizzle the cooled melted chocolate into the mixing container.

5 **Store or serve the ice cream**
The ice cream can be served immediately, but for a fuller flavor and a firmer consistency, transfer the ice cream to a plastic freezer container, cover tightly, and freeze until firm, at least 3 hours or up to 3 days.

# Pumpkin Ice Cream

Fresh pumpkin purée can be used for this ice cream, but a good-quality canned purée is easier and will yield more consistent results. The flavor of this ice cream is like frozen pumpkin pie, infused with caramel-like brown sugar and warm spices. Top with a drizzle of Caramel Sauce (page 26), if you like.

1 **Prepare the custard ingredients**
Put 1½ cups (12 fl oz/375 ml) of the cream, the brown sugar, and the molasses in a medium saucepan. In a small bowl, whisk together the egg yolks, cinnamon, nutmeg, ginger, and the remaining ½ cup (4 fl oz/125 ml) cream until they are well blended and smooth.

2 **Temper the egg yolks and cook the custard**
To find out more about tempering eggs, turn to page 35. Place the saucepan over medium heat and cook, stirring frequently with a wooden spoon, until bubbles form around the edges, the liquid just begins to ripple in the center, and the sugar is dissolved, 4–5 minutes. Do not allow to come to a boil. Begin whisking the egg yolk mixture while slowly pouring one-fourth of the hot cream mixture into the yolks. When one-fourth of the hot liquid has been added, slowly pour the warmed yolk mixture back into the saucepan, whisking constantly until well blended. Place the saucepan over medium heat and stir constantly until the mixture has thickened, 4–5 minutes.

3 **Strain the custard and add the pumpkin**
Set a fine-mesh sieve over a medium bowl. Pour the hot custard through the sieve, gently pressing the liquid through the sieve into the bowl and leaving any grainy solids in the sieve. Stir in the pumpkin purée and vanilla extract.

4 **Chill the custard**
Fill a large mixing bowl halfway with ice cubes and enough cold water just to cover the ice cubes. Place the bowl with the custard into the larger bowl and let cool for 30–45 minutes. Remove the bowl with the custard and place a piece of plastic wrap directly onto the surface of the custard and on top of the bowl. Refrigerate for 3 hours or up to 24 hours.

5 **Churn the ice cream**
Prepare an ice cream maker with at least a 1-quart (1-l) capacity according to the manufacturer's directions. Remove the plastic wrap from the custard and bowl, pour into the ice cream maker, and churn. About 1 minute before the end of the churning time, add the rum, if you are using it.

6 **Store or serve the ice cream**
The ice cream can be served immediately, but for a fuller flavor and a firmer consistency, transfer the ice cream to a plastic freezer container, cover tightly, and freeze until firm, at least 3 hours or up to 3 days.

2 cups (16 fl oz/500 ml) heavy (double) cream

⅔ cup (5 oz/155 g) firmly packed dark brown sugar

2 tablespoons light molasses

5 large egg yolks (page 34)

½ teaspoon ground cinnamon

½ teaspoon freshly grated nutmeg

½ teaspoon ground ginger

1 cup (8 oz/250 g) fresh or canned unsweetened pumpkin purée

1 teaspoon vanilla extract (essence)

1 tablespoon dark rum, optional

MAKES ABOUT 1 QUART (1 L)

**PASTRY CHEF'S TIP**
*Don't mistake canned pumpkin-pie filling, which is sweetened and contains various spices, for pure pumpkin purée. The packaging looks similar and the cans are usually stacked next to one another on the grocer's shelf.*

# Philadelphia-Style Vanilla Ice Cream

Ice cream made by simply churning milk, cream, sugar, and flavorings is variously known as Philadelphia, American, or New York style. It is far quicker and easier to prepare than French-style ice cream because it doesn't require making a custard. It is a great choice for serving on ice cream cones.

2 cups (16 fl oz/500 ml) heavy (double) cream

1 cup (8 fl oz/250 ml) whole milk

¾ cup (6 oz/185 g) granulated sugar

1 tablespoon vanilla extract (essence)

MAKES ABOUT 1 QUART (1 L)

**PASTRY CHEF'S TIP**

*Even though it seems that the ice cream will be richer, do not attempt to make it with heavy (double) cream alone. The higher percentage of butterfat in the cream tends to solidify, causing a flaky or grainy texture.*

1 **Prepare the ice cream mixture**
In a bowl, stir together the cream and milk. Add the sugar and whisk until the sugar is dissolved, 3–4 minutes. Test for graininess by tasting a small amount of the liquid; it should feel smooth on the tongue and there should be no sugar visible on the bottom of the bowl when it is stirred or spooned out. Continue whisking, if necessary, to ensure that the texture of the finished ice cream will be smooth. Stir in the vanilla extract.

2 **Chill the ice cream mixture**
Fill a large mixing bowl halfway with ice cubes and enough cold water just to cover the ice cubes. Place the bowl with the cream mixture into the larger bowl and let cool for 30–45 minutes. Remove the bowl with the cream mixture and place a piece of plastic wrap directly onto the surface and on top of the bowl. Refrigerate for 3 hours or up to 24 hours.

3 **Churn the ice cream**
Prepare an ice cream maker with at least a 1-quart (1-l) capacity according to the manufacturer's directions. Remove the plastic wrap from the cream mixture and bowl. Pour the well-chilled cream mixture into the mixing container of the ice cream maker and freeze according to the manufacturer's directions. The timing will depend on the type of machine and the temperature of the cream mixture.

4 **Store or serve the ice cream**
The ice cream can be served immediately, directly from the mixing container, but it will have a very soft consistency and a mild flavor. For a fuller flavor and a firmer consistency, use a rubber spatula to transfer the ice cream to a plastic freezer container. Cover tightly and freeze until the ice cream is firm, at least 3 hours or up to 2 days. The ice cream is at its best when served within 12 hours of freezing. (Philadelphia-style ice cream tends to become grainy more quickly and is best eaten within a day or two of churning.)

# Pistachio Gelato

Made with a higher egg-to-cream ratio than other custard-based ice creams, this typical Italian gelato is dense and intensely flavored. The appealing flavor, natural green color, and wonderful crunch of pistachios make them an ideal addition. The resulting gelato is aromatic and creamy.

1 **Shell the pistachio nuts**
Pull apart the shell halves and transfer the nutmeats to a bowl. This process is a little tedious, but it's well worth it for the flavor the fresh nuts contribute.

2 **Remove the nut skins**
Use your fingertips to pour the nuts into a folded kitchen towel. Then, use the towel to rub off as much of the light brown skin covering the nuts as possible. You can also use your fingers for this step.

3 **Make the pistachio paste**
In a food processor, combine half of the pistachios and ¼ cup (2 oz/60 g) of the sugar. Pulse to chop the nuts coarsely, then process until the nuts are finely ground to a rough paste, about 1 minute. Stop the processor a few times and scrape down the sides of the work bowl with a rubber spatula.

4 **Chop the remaining nuts**
Place the remaining nuts on a cutting board. Using a chef's knife and an up-and-down motion, coarsely chop the nuts. Do not use the food processor for this step; it will chop the nuts unevenly and create a lot of nut "dust" that will make the ice cream grainy.

5 **Separate the eggs**
If you need help separating eggs, turn to page 34. Have ready 2 small bowls and 1 larger heatproof glass or stainless-steel bowl. Holding an egg in your hand, strike it sharply on its equator on the work surface, cracking it, then hold it upright over 1 small bowl and lift away the top half of the shell. The yolk should be resting in the bottom half. Working gently so as not to break the yolk, transfer the yolk back and forth between the shell halves over the bowl, allowing all the egg white to drop into the bowl. Drop the yolk into the second small bowl and transfer the white to the larger metal bowl. Repeat with the remaining 5 eggs. Set the yolks aside. Reserve the whites for another use, such as Individual Baked Alaskas (page 113).

6 **Prepare the custard ingredients**
Put the cream, egg yolks, and remaining ½ cup (4 oz/125 g) sugar in a medium bowl. Using a whisk, vigorously mix together the ingredients until they are blended and a slightly pale, buttery yellow, about 2–3 minutes.

1½ cups (6 oz/185 g) unsalted whole pistachio nuts

¾ cup (6 oz/185 g) granulated sugar

6 large eggs

1 cup (8 fl oz/250 ml) heavy (double) cream

2 cups (16 fl oz/500 ml) whole milk

2 teaspoons vanilla extract (essence)

MAKES ABOUT 1 QUART (1 L)

**CHEF'S TIP**
*If you buy pistachios in the shell, look for shells that are partially open, which makes removal of the shell easier and also signifies a mature nut. Avoid nuts that are artificially colored red and those that are salted.*

By infusing the custard base with the natural color of the pistachios, the finished ice cream will be an appealing green.

## 7 Temper the egg yolks

Put the milk in a medium saucepan. Scrape in the pistachio paste, stirring to distribute the paste throughout the milk. Place the saucepan over medium heat and cook, stirring frequently with a wooden spoon, until bubbles form around the edges, the liquid just begins to ripple in the center, and the sugar is dissolved, 3–5 minutes. Do not allow the milk to come to a boil, or the mixture may scorch. Remove the pan from the heat. Begin whisking the egg yolk mixture with one hand while slowly pouring one-fourth of the hot milk into the yolks with the other. This method of slowly adding a hot liquid to egg yolks is called *tempering;* if the liquid is added too quickly, the yolks will get too hot and begin to scramble. When one-fourth of the hot milk mixture has been blended into the yolks, slowly pour the warmed yolk mixture back into the saucepan, whisking constantly until well blended. To find out more about tempering eggs, turn to page 35.

## 8 Cook the custard

Place the saucepan with the milk-and-yolk mixture over medium heat and cook, stirring constantly with a wooden spoon, for 4–5 minutes. As you stir, make sure you reach all areas on the bottom of the saucepan to ensure that the custard does not scorch or curdle. The custard should come to a bare simmer, with steam rising from the surface and the surface ripling, but it should not reach a boil. It is ready when it is thick enough to coat the back of the spoon, and if you draw your finger along the spoon, it leaves a trail that does not fill in immediately. The custard will appear grainy because of the pistachio paste.

## 9 Strain the custard

Set a fine-mesh sieve over a medium mixing bowl. Pour the hot custard through the sieve, pressing firmly on the solids to extract as much liquid as possible. Discard the solids. Stir the vanilla extract into the custard.

## 10 Chill the custard

Fill a large mixing bowl halfway with ice cubes and enough water just to cover the ice cubes. Place the bowl with the custard into the larger bowl, nestling the medium bowl into the ice cubes. Let the custard cool, stirring occasionally, until it reaches room temperature, 30–45 minutes. Once the custard has cooled to room temperature, remove the medium bowl from the ice-water bath. Place a piece of plastic wrap directly on the surface of the custard, which will prevent a coating, or "skin," from forming. Cover the top of the bowl with plastic wrap and refrigerate until the custard is well chilled, at least 3 hours or up to 24 hours. A well-chilled custard will freeze more effectively and have a better flavor.

### 11 Churn the gelato

Remove the plastic wrap from the bowl and the custard. A coating, or "skin," may cling to the wrap. Leave it on the wrap and discard. Prepare an ice cream maker with at least a 1-quart (1-l) capacity according to the manufacturer's directions. Pour the well-chilled custard into the mixing container of the ice cream maker and churn until the gelato is the consistency of dense, thick whipped cream. The timing will depend on the type of machine you are using and the temperature of the custard.

### 12 Add the pistachios

When the gelato is nearly finished churning, add the coarsely chopped pistachios. Continue to churn until the nuts are distributed evenly throughout, about 1 minute. If the nuts jam the paddle, turn the machine off and use a rubber spatula to stir in the nuts by hand.

### 13 Store the gelato

The gelato can be served immediately, directly from the mixing container, but it will have a very soft consistency and mild flavor. For fuller flavor and a firmer consistency, use a rubber spatula to transfer the gelato to a plastic freezer container. Cover tightly and freeze until the gelato is firm, at least 3 hours or up to 3 days. It is best served 6 to 12 hours after being transferred to the freezer.

### 14 Serve the gelato

To serve the gelato, dip an ice cream scoop into hot water and warm briefly. Pull the scoop across the gelato to form a rounded scoop. For more details on how to scoop gelato, turn to page 42. Store any remaining gelato, tightly covered, in the freezer.

## Serving ideas

*Because of its dense texture and full flavor, gelato needs little embellishment. A sprinkle of chopped nuts contributes another layer of flavor and a pleasant crunch to a scoop or two in a small dish. Placing small scoops of gelato in miniature paper cups displayed on a decorative platter is an easy way to serve a crowd. Finally, adding dried cranberries along with nuts to the gelato as it finishes churning gives it a festive, colorful look.*

**Chopped pistachio garnish** (top left)
If you like the flavor and texture of nuts in your gelato, top each serving with a scattering of chopped pistachios.

**Gelato balls** (left)
Arrange miniature muffin cup liners on a rimmed baking sheet. As you form each small scoop of gelato, place it in a paper liners, then place the baking sheet in the freezer for 10 minutes. Serve the balls on a decorative platter.

**Pistachio gelato with cranberries** (above)
Add ½ cup (2 oz/60 g) coarsely chopped dried cranberries at the same time you add the coarsely chopped nuts to the gelato.

## White Chocolate Gelato

Here, the typically dense, smooth, luxurious character of gelato is enhanced by the use of white chocolate, which has a mild chocolate flavor and boasts a high percentage of cocoa butter. The addition of vanilla extract and orange-flower water to the creamy-colored gelato imparts floral accents that nicely balance the richness of the chocolate, cream, and egg yolks.

2 cups (16 fl oz/500 ml) whole milk

1 cup (8 fl oz/250 ml) heavy (double) cream

½ cup (4 oz/125 g) granulated sugar

6 large egg yolks (page 34)

4 oz (125 g) white chocolate, chopped (page 36)

1 teaspoon vanilla extract (essence)

1 tablespoon orange-flower water or rose water, optional

MAKES ABOUT 1 QUART (1 L)

**PASTRY CHEF'S TIP**

*When purchasing white chocolate, read the label carefully. If cocoa butter is not included in the list of ingredients, or if the words* artificial, confectionary coating, *or* chocolate flavored *are included, the white chocolate is inferior and probably will not melt well. Similarly, white chocolate chips are designed to hold their shape during baking and will not melt successfully.*

1 **Prepare the custard ingredients**
Put the milk, ½ cup (4 fl oz/125 ml) of the cream, and the sugar in a medium saucepan. In a small bowl, whisk together the egg yolks and the remaining ½ cup (4 fl oz/125 ml) cream until blended.

2 **Temper the egg yolks**
Place the saucepan over medium heat and cook, stirring with a wooden spoon, until bubbles form around the edges, the liquid just begins to ripple in the center, and the sugar is dissolved, 4–5 minutes. Do not allow to come to a boil. To find out more about tempering eggs, turn to page 35. Begin whisking the yolks while slowly pouring one-fourth of the hot milk mixture into the yolks. When one-fourth of the hot liquid has been added, slowly pour the yolk mixture back into the saucepan, whisking constantly until blended. Place the saucepan over medium heat and stir constantly until the mixture has thickened, 4–5 minutes.

3 **Add the white chocolate and strain the custard**
Remove the pan from the heat. Sprinkle the chopped white chocolate over the top of the custard and let stand for 1 minute. Stir gently until the chocolate is melted and the custard is smooth, about 2 minutes. Stir in the vanilla extract and the flower water, if using, until blended. Set a fine-mesh sieve over a medium mixing bowl. Pour the hot custard through the sieve, gently pressing the liquid through the sieve into the bowl and leaving any grainy solids in the sieve.

4 **Chill the custard**
Fill a large mixing bowl halfway with ice cubes and enough cold water just to cover the ice cubes. Place the bowl with the custard into the larger bowl and let cool for 30–45 minutes. Remove the bowl with custard and place a piece of plastic wrap directly onto the surface of the custard and on top of the bowl. Refrigerate for 3 hours or up to 24 hours.

5 **Churn the gelato**
Prepare an ice cream maker according to the manufacturer's directions. Remove the plastic wrap from the custard, pour into the mixing container of the ice cream maker, and churn until it is the consistency of a thick whipped cream.

6 **Store or serve the gelato**
The ice cream can be served immediately, but for a fuller flavor and a firmer consistency, transfer the gelato to a plastic freezer container, cover tightly, and freeze for at least 3 hours or up to 3 days.

# Buttermilk Sherbet

The naturally thick character of buttermilk gives this sherbet both a lush texture and a lemony tang that is heightened by a small amount of lemon juice. Buttermilk is lower in fat than cream or whole milk, which makes this sherbet a good choice when you want something cold and rich tasting, but don't want the calories of ice cream.

1 cup (8 fl oz/250 ml) water

1⅓ cups (11 oz/340 g) granulated sugar

1 tablespoon fresh lemon juice

2 cups (16 fl oz/500 ml) well-chilled low-fat buttermilk

2 teaspoons vanilla extract (essence)

MAKES ABOUT 1 QUART (1 L)

## 1 Prepare the sugar syrup

Put the water and sugar in a medium saucepan. Place the pan over medium heat and cook, stirring constantly with a wooden spoon, until the mixture comes just to a boil with bubbles beginning to pop in the center, 4–5 minutes. The syrup should be clear, with no undissolved grains of sugar. If it is not, the sherbet will have a coarse texture. Remove the pan from the heat, stir in the lemon juice, and let the syrup cool to room temperature, 30–45 minutes. (The syrup can also be prepared up to 24 hours in advance and refrigerated until ready to use.)

## 2 Prepare the sherbet mixture

Fresh buttermilk separates in the container, with the watery liquid rising to the top and the thick milk product settling to the bottom. Before pouring and measuring the buttermilk, shake the container for at least 15 seconds to recombine it. Put the buttermilk and vanilla extract in a medium bowl. Add the syrup and stir to blend. Cover the bowl with plastic wrap and refrigerate the mixture until well chilled, at least 1 hour or up to 8 hours.

## 3 Churn the sherbet

Prepare an ice cream maker with at least a 1-quart (1-l) capacity according to the manufacturer's directions. Pour the buttermilk mixture into the ice cream maker and churn until the ice cream is the consistency of thick whipped cream.

## 4 Store or serve the sherbet

The sherbet can be served right away; it will have a very smooth texture. For a firmer texture and a tangier flavor, transfer the sherbet to a plastic freezer container, cover tightly, and freeze until the sherbet is firm, at least 3 hours or up to 2 days.

**PASTRY CHEF'S TIP**

*If you use a lot of vanilla extract (essence), making your own saves money and allows you to control the flavor better. Cut a whole vanilla bean in half lengthwise and place both halves in a glass jar with ¾ cup (6 fl oz/180 ml) vodka. Cap tightly and store in a cool, dark place for 6 months before using.*

# 4

# Sorbet
# & Granita

Vibrant-colored sorbets and granitas are quite easy to make and, like most of the recipes in this book, call for only a few basic ingredients. They are typically made by combining a simple sugar syrup and a fruit purée or other flavoring such as chocolate, and are a great way to showcase the cool and refreshing flavors of ripe fresh fruits in eye-catching presentations.

# Mango Sorbet

Like most sorbets, this one contains no eggs or dairy products—nothing to dilute the intense flavor of the main ingredient. Fruits with assertive flavors and bright colors, like the mango used here, are the best choices for sorbet. Make this sorbet in summer, when mangoes are easily found in the market.

## 1 Pit the mango

To tell if a mango is ripe, it should give off a strong aroma at the stem end, give slightly to pressure, and have perfectly smooth skin. Look for mangoes that have a yellow tint, as they tend to be the most flavorful. Mangoes have a large, flat pit in the center, about the shape and size of your palm. The best way to work with the fruit is to first slice it from the pit. To pit the mango, stand it up on its narrow side, with the stem end facing away from you. Using a chef's knife, cut down the length of the fruit, about 1 inch (2.5 cm) from the stem and just grazing the pit. Repeat on the other side of the pit. You should now have 2 halves. If desired, trim off the flesh left encircling the pit and discard the pit.

## 2 Score the mango

Place one mango half, cut side up, on a cutting board. Using a paring knife, make several cuts about ½ inch (12 mm) apart in a crisscross pattern in the mango flesh, stopping just short of the skin. This is known as *scoring*.

## 3 Cut the mango into cubes

With both hands, hold the scored mango half from the skin side and push up to expose cubes of mango flesh. Then, using the paring knife, carefully cut across the base of the cubes to free them, letting them fall into a bowl. Repeat the scoring and cutting steps with the remaining mango half. (Alternatively, after the mango has been pitted, use a paring knife to cut each half into 4 large strips. Cut the skin from each strip. Then, cut each strip crosswise into cubes.) Set the cubes aside. Repeat the process with the other mango. ›

2 large, ripe mangoes, about 2 lb (1 kg) total weight

⅔ cup (5 oz/155 g) granulated sugar

¾ cup (6 fl oz/180 ml) mango nectar or water

1½ tablespoons fresh lime juice

1 tablespoon rum or brandy, optional

MAKES ABOUT 1 QUART (1 L)

**PASTRY CHEF'S TIP**
*If you have underripe mangoes (mangoes that are firm to the touch), place them in a paper bag and keep at room temperature for 2–3 days to encourage ripening.*

### 4 Prepare the mango syrup

Measure out ⅔ cup (5 oz/155 g) sugar, then taste a mango cube. If the mango is very sweet, decrease the sugar by 1 tablespoon. Put the sugar and mango nectar in a small saucepan. Stir with a wooden spoon to combine the ingredients. The mixture will look cloudy and grainy. Place over medium-high heat, stir with a wooden spoon, and bring to a boil, 3–4 minutes. You want bubbles rising and breaking all over the surface. Stirring frequently, boil the syrup until it is clear and there are no visible grains of sugar, 1–2 minutes. Even a small amount of undissolved sugar can cause the sorbet to be grainy, so watch carefully and don't remove the mixture from the heat too soon. Remove from the heat and set aside.

### 5 Juice the limes

Press and roll the lime firmly against a countertop to break some of the membranes holding in the juice. Then, using a chef's knife, cut the fruit in half crosswise. Have ready a small bowl to catch the juice. To extract as much juice as possible, use a citrus reamer to pierce the membranes as you squeeze, capturing the juice in the bowl. Strain to remove the seeds before using. Set aside. For more details on juicing citrus fruits, turn to page 40.

### 6 Purée the mango with the syrup

Add the mango cubes to a food processor along with ⅓ cup (3 fl oz/80 ml) of the warm mango syrup. Turn on the machine and let it run, stopping occasionally to scrape down the sides of the work bowl with a rubber spatula, until the mixture is evenly puréed and pale orange, about 1 minute.

### 7 Chill the purée

Pour the mango purée into a medium bowl. If the mango was very sweet when you tasted it, stir in 1 tablespoon of the lime juice; if it tasted slightly sweet, stir in the entire 1½ tablespoons. The lime juice will help intensify the mango flavor. Cover the bowl with plastic wrap and refrigerate the purée until it is very cold, at least 3 hours or up to 8 hours. ›

**PASTRY CHEF'S TIP**

*If fresh mangoes are out of season, buy them frozen, already peeled and diced, from the market. Let thaw to room temperature.*

## 8 Churn the sorbet

Prepare an ice cream maker with at least a 1-quart (1-l) capacity according to the manufacturer's directions. Pour the well-chilled mango purée into the mixing container of the ice cream maker and churn according to the manufacturer's directions. The timing will depend on the type of machine you are using and the temperature of the purée. When the sorbet is almost finished churning and it has thickened and mounds on the paddle, add the rum, if using. Rum nicely complements the mango, lending a tropical flavor. The rum is added near the end of the churning process so that the alcohol does not inhibit freezing. Continue to churn until the sorbet is smooth and mounds again, 1–2 minutes.

  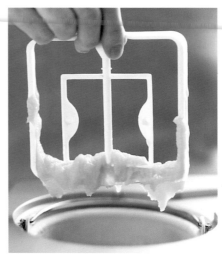 

**PASTRY CHEF'S TIP**

*Sorbets with a high concentration of sugar, either granulated or naturally occurring, will not freeze as solid as those with a lower concentration, but they will have a smoother, richer texture. The amount of sugar given here is a good guideline to follow, but if the fruit is too tart or sweet, adjust the amount up or down by 1–2 tablespoons.*

## 9 Store the sorbet

The sorbet can be served immediately, directly from the mixing container, when it is soft but has an intensely fruity flavor. For a firmer consistency, use a rubber spatula to transfer the sorbet to a plastic freezer container. Cover tightly and freeze until the sorbet is firm, at least 3 hours or up to 2 days. It is best served within 6–12 hours.

## 10 Serve the sorbet

Scoop the sorbet, storing any remaining sorbet, tightly covered, in the freezer for up to 2 days. For more details on how to scoop sorbet, turn to page 42.

## Serving ideas

*Sorbets are usually richly colored, making them attractive desserts for nearly any occasion. Layering sorbet with whipped cream is an elegant and easy dinner-party dessert. For a contrast in texture and flavor, serve scoops of sorbet with scoops of ice cream that have been rolled in toasted coconut. Or, top scoops of sorbet with warm chocolate sauce for an interesting twist on a hot fudge sundae.*

**Sorbet parfait** (top left)
Layer dollops of Sweetened Whipped Cream (page 30) between scoops of sorbet in tall, footed glasses.

**Mango–coconut bonbon sundae** (left)
Line a small rimmed baking sheet with waxed paper. Use a small ice cream scoop to make scoops of Coconut Ice Cream (page 53) and place on the baking sheet. Place the baking sheet in the freezer for 10 minutes. Remove from the freezer and roll each ball in toasted flaked coconut. Pair with small scoops of Mango Sorbet (page 81) in a bowl.

**Chocolate-mango sundae** (above)
Drizzle warm Chocolate Sauce (page 24) over small scoops of Mango Sorbet (page 81) in a bowl.

# Fruit Sorbet Variations

The steps you mastered for making Mango Sorbet (page 81)—peeling and puréeing the fruit, making the syrup, churning the chilled purée—can now be applied to many other fruit flavors, including the six suggested here. For the best results, always start with boldly flavored fruits or fruit juices, whether bright yellow peaches or scarlet raspberries, tart and juicy green apples or freshly squeezed orange juice. If you are putting the sorbet in the freezer directly after making it, allow it to warm and soften slightly before serving. The flavor will be fuller and the sorbet will be easier to scoop. Each variation makes 1 quart (1 l) sorbet.

## Peach Sorbet

Be sure to buy ripe, slightly soft peaches for this summer sorbet. If you want to make it at other times of the year, use good-quality frozen peaches.

Make a peach syrup: In a saucepan, stir together 1 cup (8 oz/250 g) granulated sugar and ¾ cup (6 fl oz/180 ml) peach or apricot nectar. Place over medium-high heat and bring to a steady boil. Boil, stirring frequently, until the syrup is clear with no visible grains of sugar, 1–2 minutes. Remove from the heat.

Add 1½ pounds (750 g) peeled (page 42) and coarsely chopped peaches to a food processor along with ⅓ cup (3 fl oz/80 ml) of the warm peach syrup. Process, stopping occasionally to scrape down the sides of the work bowl with a rubber spatula, until evenly puréed, about 1 minute. Pour the purée into a bowl and stir in 1½ tablespoons fresh lemon juice. Cover and refrigerate until very cold, 3–8 hours.

Pour the chilled peach purée into the ice cream maker and churn according to the manufacturer's directions. If desired, add 1 tablespoon brandy or rum near the end of the churning process, then store or serve the sorbet.

## Lemon Sorbet

If you want to use Meyer lemons, which are particularly fragrant and sweeter than the more common Eureka lemons, decrease the sugar in the syrup by ¼ cup (2 fl oz/60 ml).

Make a lemon syrup: In a medium saucepan, stir together 1 cup (8 oz/250 g) granulated sugar and 1 cup (8 fl oz/250 ml) water. Place over medium-high heat and bring to a steady boil. Boil, stirring frequently, until the syrup is clear with no visible grains of sugar, 1–2 minutes. Remove from the heat and stir in 1 tablespoon grated lemon zest. Let cool to room temperature, about 30 minutes. Stir 1¼ cups (10 fl oz/310 ml) fresh lemon juice into the syrup. Pour into a bowl, cover, and refrigerate until very cold, 3–8 hours.

Pour the chilled lemon mixture into the ice cream maker and churn according the manufacturer's directions, then store or serve the sorbet.

## Orange Sorbet

For the best sorbet, begin with fresh orange juice that you squeezed yourself, or buy the juice from a grocer that makes it fresh daily. In either case, be sure that the oranges are very flavorful.

In a bowl, stir together 2½ cups (20 fl oz/ 625 ml) room-temperature orange juice (from about 6 oranges), 1 tablespoon fresh lemon juice, ¾ cup (6 oz/185 g) granulated sugar, and 1 tablespoon grated orange zest until the sugar is dissolved and the liquid no longer feels or appears grainy, 10–15 minutes (this syrup is not heated, which would cause orange juice to lose some of its fresh flavor). Pour into a bowl. The sorbet will have an intense flavor and interesting texture if left unstrained, but if you prefer a more subtle flavor and a perfectly smooth texture, strain the liquid through a fine-mesh sieve. Cover and refrigerate the orange mixture until very cold, 3–8 hours.

Pour the chilled orange mixture into the ice cream maker and churn according to the manufacturer's directions. If desired, add 1 tablespoon Grand Marnier, near the end of the churning process, then store or serve the sorbet.

# Raspberry Sorbet

If good, fresh raspberries are not available, high-quality unsweetened frozen berries can be substituted.

Make a sugar syrup: In a saucepan, stir together **1 cup (8 oz/250 g) granulated sugar** and **1 cup (8 fl oz/250 ml) water**. Place over medium-high heat and bring to a steady boil. Boil, stirring frequently, until the syrup is clear with no visible grains of sugar, 1–2 minutes. Add **4 cups (1 lb/500 g) raspberries** and return to a boil. Reduce the heat to medium-low and simmer gently, stirring constantly, until the berries are very soft, 1–2 minutes.

Slowly pour the mixture through a fine-mesh sieve into a heatproof bowl, pressing hard on the berries with the back of a large metal spoon. Push as much fruit purée through the sieve as possible. If the seeds clog the sieve, use a rubber spatula to scrape them out and then discard. Let cool to room temperature, 10–15 minutes. Stir in **1 tablespoon fresh lemon juice**. Cover and refrigerate until very cold, 3–8 hours.

Pour the chilled purée into the ice cream maker and churn according to the manufacturer's directions. If desired, add **1 tablespoon raspberry liqueur or syrup** near the end of the churning process, then store or serve the sorbet.

> **PASTRY CHEF'S TIP**
> *Berries should always be rinsed just before using, but don't soak them in water, or they will absorb it. After rinsing, spread berries on paper towels to drain.*

# Green Apple Sorbet

The apple purée will not be completely smooth, so this sorbet will have a coarser texture than most. Tart green apples, such as Granny Smith, work best here. Choose a high-quality unsweetened cider to make the syrup.

Make an apple syrup: In a saucepan, stir together **1 cup (8 oz/250 g) granulated sugar** and **1¼ cups (10 fl oz/310 ml) apple cider**. Place over medium-high heat and bring to a steady boil. Boil, stirring frequently, until the syrup is clear with no visible grains of sugar, 1–2 minutes.

Add **1 lb (500 g) peeled, cored, and coarsely chopped tart green apples** and return to a boil. Reduce the heat to medium-low and cook, stirring constantly, until the apples are softened and mushy, 3–5 minutes. Let cool to room temperature, 10–15 minutes.

Stir in **1 tablespoon fresh lemon juice**. Use a slotted spoon to transfer the soft apples to a food processor. Pour in 1 cup (8 fl oz/ 250 ml) of the cooking liquid, then process to make a fairly smooth purée, about 30 seconds. Transfer the puréed apples and the remaining cooking liquid to a bowl and stir to combine. Cover and refrigerate until very cold, 3–8 hours.

Pour the chilled purée into the ice cream maker and churn according to the manufacturer's directions. If desired, add **1 tablespoon Calvados or brandy** near the end of the churning process, then store or serve the sorbet.

# Plum Sorbet

There are two ways to make this sorbet: with unstrained plum purée for a coarser texture or with strained plum purée for a smooth texture.

Make a plum syrup: In a medium saucepan, stir together **⅔ cup (5 oz/155 g) granulated sugar** and **½ cup (4 fl oz/125 ml) prune (dried plum) juice**. Place over medium-high heat and bring to a steady boil. Boil, stirring frequently, until the syrup is clear with no visible grains of sugar, 1–2 minutes.

Add **2 lb (1 kg) pitted and coarsely chopped plums** and return to a boil. Reduce the heat to medium-low and cook, stirring constantly, until the plums are soft and mushy, 2–3 minutes. Let cool to room temperature, 10–15 minutes.

In 2 batches, transfer the plum mixture to a food processor and process to make a fairly smooth purée, about 30 seconds. If you prefer a smooth texture, strain the purée through a fine-mesh sieve. Scrape the purée into a bowl, cover, and refrigerate until very cold, 3–8 hours.

Pour the chilled purée into the ice cream maker and churn according to the manufacturer's directions. If desired, add **1 tablespoon rum or crème de cassis** near the end of the churning process, then store or serve the sorbet.

# Chocolate Sorbet

Using both unsweetened cocoa and bittersweet or semisweet chocolate gives this sorbet an intense chocolate flavor. Because sorbet does not contain eggs or dairy products, the chocolate flavor here is particularly rich and bold. The addition of the espresso powder and coffee liqueur gives the sorbet a wonderful mocha flavor.

1 cup (8 oz/250 g) granulated sugar

¾ cup (2½ oz/75 g) unsweetened nonalkalized cocoa powder

2 cups (16 fl oz/500 ml) water

2 oz (60 g) bittersweet or semisweet (plain) chocolate, chopped (page 36)

2 teaspoons vanilla extract (essence)

1 tablespoon instant espresso powder, optional

1 tablespoon Kahlúa or other coffee liqueur, coffee syrup, or clear crème de menthe, optional

MAKES ABOUT 1 QUART (1 LITER)

**PASTRY CHEF'S TIP**

*Cocoa powder often forms clumps when combined with a liquid. If you mix it with sugar first, however, the cocoa grains will separate and are more likely to remain that way. If the cocoa still clumps a bit after you add the water, keep whisking while you heat the cocoa-sugar syrup and the lumps will eventually dissolve.*

1 **Prepare the cocoa sugar syrup**
Put the sugar and cocoa in a medium saucepan. Use a wire whisk to stir the sugar and cocoa together. Slowly whisk in the water to make a smooth mixture, with no lumps of cocoa remaining. Place over medium-high heat, stir with a wooden spoon, and bring to a boil, 3–4 minutes. You want bubbles rising and breaking all over the surface. Stirring frequently, boil the syrup until it is dark and smooth and there are no visible grains of sugar, 1–2 minutes.

2 **Add the chocolate to the syrup**
Remove the pan from the heat. Add the chocolate and let it stand for 1 minute so that it begins to melt, then stir with the wooden spoon until the chocolate is completely melted and the mixture is smooth and uniformly dark, 1–2 minutes. Stir in the vanilla extract and the espresso powder, if using (the espresso powder deepens the flavor), and continue stirring until smooth.

3 **Chill the chocolate mixture**
Pour the chocolate mixture into a medium bowl, scraping the sides of the pan with a rubber spatula. Let it cool to room temperature, 30–45 minutes. Cover the bowl with plastic wrap and refrigerate the mixture until it is very cold, at least 3 hours or up to 8 hours.

4 **Churn the sorbet**
Prepare an ice cream maker with at least a 1-quart (1-l) capacity according to the manufacturer's directions. Pour the well-chilled chocolate mixture into the ice cream maker and churn. The timing will depend on the type of ice cream maker and the temperature of the chocolate mixture. When the sorbet is almost finished churning and it has thickened and mounds on the paddle, add the liqueur or syrup, if using. Continue to churn until the sorbet is smooth and mounds again, 1–2 minutes.

5 **Serve or store the sorbet**
The sorbet can be served immediately, directly from the mixing container, when it is soft and richly flavored. For a firmer consistency, use a rubber spatula to transfer the sorbet to a plastic freezer container. Cover tightly and freeze until the sorbet is firm, at least 3 hours or up to 3 days. The sorbet has a little fat in it from the melted chocolate, so it will keep its texture in the freezer longer than a pure fruit sorbet. It is at its best when served within 12–24 hours.

# Watermelon Granita

Granitas are a great way to showcase ripe summer fruit, like the bright pink watermelon used here. Although the granita tastes like frozen pure watermelon, the other ingredients—dissolved sugar for texture, white grape juice for sweetness, lemon juice for freshness—also contribute to this refreshing treat.

## 1 Prepare the sugar syrup

Put the sugar and juice or water in a small saucepan. Stir with a wooden spoon to combine the ingredients. The mixture will look cloudy and grainy. Place over medium-high heat, stir with a wooden spoon, and bring to a boil, 3–4 minutes. You want bubbles rising and breaking all over the surface. Stirring frequently, boil the syrup until it is clear and there are no visible grains of sugar, 1–2 minutes. Even a small amount of undissolved sugar can cause the granita to be grainy, so watch carefully and don't remove the mixture from the heat too soon. Remove from the heat and set aside.

## 2 Chill the sugar syrup

Pour the syrup into a heatproof glass or stainless-steel bowl. Let cool to room temperature, about 20 minutes. Then, cover with plastic wrap and refrigerate the syrup until it is very cold, about 1 hour.

## 3 Cut the watermelon into wedges

While small Sugar Baby watermelons are preferred because of their size, they are not always available. The more common, larger types of watermelon you see at the store can also be used (you will have a lot left over, which can be eaten alone or used as a garnish for the granita). Starting with a cold watermelon will help the freezing process go faster. If you need help cutting the melon, turn to page 41. Using a chef's knife, cut the melon in half, then cut each half in half again to make large wedges. Next, cut the pink flesh from the pale green rind: Place 1 melon wedge on a flat surface and, using the chef's knife, gently cut the flesh from the rind. If you choose a watermelon with seeds, remove the seeds by gently scooping them out with a grapefruit spoon. If you have a seedless watermelon with clear, watery seeds, you do not need to remove the seeds.

## 4 Cut the watermelon into cubes

Lay the wedge on its side and, using the chef's knife, cut it lengthwise into strips 1 inch (12 mm) wide. Line up 2 or 3 strips and then cut crosswise into cubes. Repeat with the remaining wedges as needed until you have 4 cups (1 lb/500 g) cubes.

½ cup (4 oz/125 g) granulated sugar

½ cup (4 fl oz/125 ml) white grape juice or water

1 small watermelon (about 1 pound/500 g), preferably Sugar Baby, well chilled

1 tablespoon fresh lemon juice

1 to 2 tablespoons bourbon, optional

MAKES ABOUT 3½ CUPS (28 FL OZ/875 G)

**PASTRY CHEF'S TIP**

*Other flavorings can be added instead of bourbon to this granita. Rum will give off a light molasses flavor, while Pernod or anisette will impart a licorice flavor.*

### 5 Prepare the fruit purée

Put the watermelon cubes in the work bowl of a food processor. Turn on the machine and let it run until the watermelon turns into a pulpy liquid, about 30 seconds. The liquid should be thin, watery, and somewhat grainy. Check the consistency by scooping up a spoonful with a rubber spatula or spoon. If it seems too coarse, process for a few seconds more.

### 6 Strain the purée, if desired

You can freeze the granita now, and it will have appealing tiny pieces of watermelon throughout. If you prefer a granita that dissolves on the tongue like flavored water, strain the fruit purée: Set a colander over a bowl. Cut a piece of cheesecloth (muslin) 3 times larger than the colander. Gather the cheesecloth into a ball, rinse it in cold water, and then wring out most of the water. Line the colander with the damp cheesecloth, letting the excess hang over the edge. Pour the puréed melon into the cheesecloth-lined colander. Let the liquid drain into the bowl underneath; this will take 10–15 minutes. Lift up the cheesecloth and twist the ends together to wring out as much liquid as possible from the pulp left in the cheesecloth. Discard the pulp. The bowl will now contain the flavored liquid and no pulp from the fruit.

### 7 Freeze the granita

Stir the sugar syrup and lemon juice into the watermelon purée or strained liquid. If you are not ready to freeze the granita right away, cover the bowl and refrigerate it for up to 8 hours. When you are ready to freeze the granita, pour it into a shallow 3-quart (3-l) metal pan, such as a 9-by-13-inch (23-by-33-cm) baking pan. Cover the pan with aluminum foil, then carefully place it in the freezer. The back and lowest parts of your freezer are the coldest, so put the pan in one of these areas to hasten freezing. Place the pan directly on the freezer rack or on the floor of the freezer so that the liquid won't spill. Freeze the purée or liquid without stirring until a thin layer of ice forms on the surface and the edges begin to harden about ½ inch (12 mm) in from the sides, about 1 hour. ›

**PASTRY CHEF'S TIP**

*To speed up the granita-making process, chill the metal pan in the freezer for up to an hour before adding the fruit purée to it.*

### 8 Break up the ice crystals

Carefully remove the pan from the freezer and remove the foil. Using a sturdy dinner fork, run the tines across the surface of the granita, breaking up any frozen areas into small shards. Mix the ice shards back into the liquid. Cover the pan and freeze again for about 30 minutes, then repeat the scraping and mixing procedure. Do this 3 or 4 times, for a total of about 2½ hours freezing time. Each time the granita will have more ice and less liquid. At the end of the freezing time, it should be icy and grainy throughout and no longer mushy.

### 9 Mix in the bourbon, if desired

About 2 hours after putting the granita into the freezer the initial time, pour the bourbon evenly over the surface of the granita and mix it in thoroughly with the fork. The bourbon will add a smokey, whisky-like flavor, a nice complement to watermelon. You must add the liquor to the granita near the end of freezing. If added earlier, the alcohol will inhibit the formation of ice crystals.

### 10 Adjust the consistency, if needed

If the granita freezes too long or you aren't able to serve it on the day it is made, you can salvage it by thawing it until it is slushy and then beginning the freezing and scraping process again. A nearly frozen granita can be broken up into chunks and processed in a food processor, though the texture won't be quite as even and icy as it would be if you scraped it by hand during alternate freezing and scraping steps.

### 11 Serve the granita

Serve the granita immediately, if possible, or keep frozen in the metal pan or scrape into a plastic freezer container with at least a 1-quart (1-l) capacity. Cover tightly and freeze for no longer than 24 hours; granita is at its best if served within 4 hours of freezing. If frozen longer than that, it can harden and lose its characteristic iciness.

# Serving Ideas

*Brightly colored and boldly flavored, a granita makes a light and refreshing finish to a meal. But dessert is not the only time to serve this icy creation. A small amount spooned into a shot glass is an ideal palate refresher between the courses at a dinner party. Layering different flavors of granita in tall glasses is a colorful presentation. So, too, is adding a garnish of a few thin slices of fresh fruit, such as strawberries, on top.*

**Granita served in shot glasses** (top left)
Fill shot glasses with granita and serve as a palate cleanser between courses of a multicourse meal.

**Granita trio** (left)
For contrasting colors, layer scoops of Watermelon Granita (page 91), with granitas made from cantaloupe and honeydew melon (page 96) in tall glasses. Be sure to provide long spoons.

**Granita garnished with fruit** (above)
Scoop granita into a clear glass or other decorative serving bowl. Garnish with a complementary fresh fruit, such as thinly sliced strawberries. Add the fruit just before serving, so that it doesn't freeze while sitting on the granita.

# Granita Variations

Once you know how to make Watermelon Granita (page 91), you will be ready to make this icy dessert from a variety of other juices, flavored syrups, or thin purées. Fruit and fruit juices, such as the melon, grapefruit, pomegranate, and apple included here, are natural choices, but espresso and a fresh mint–infused syrup also make delicious granitas. The secret to success is to use the right quantity of dissolved sugar to achieve the correct consistency of granular ice shards. Too little sugar and the liquid will simply freeze into an ice cube; too much sugar and it won't freeze at all. Each variation makes 3½ cups (28 fl oz/875 ml) granita.

## Melon Granita

Melon season usually occurs during the hottest months of the year, which is also a good time to make refreshing granitas.

Make a sugar syrup: In a small saucepan, stir together ½ cup (4 oz/125 g) granulated sugar and ½ cup (4 fl oz/125 ml) white grape juice or water. Place over medium-high heat and bring to a steady boil. Boil, stirring frequently, until the syrup is clear, with no visible grains of sugar, 1–2 minutes. Remove from the heat, pour into a heatproof bowl, and let cool to room temperature, about 20 minutes. Cover and refrigerate until the syrup is very cold, about 1 hour.

In a food processor, process 4 cups (1 lb/500 g) ripe cantaloupe or honeydew chunks (page 41) until smooth, about 1 minute. For a very smooth (but slightly less flavorful) granita, strain the melon purée through a colander lined with cheesecloth (muslin) placed over a bowl. Stir in the cold syrup and 1 tablespoon fresh lime juice.

Proceed with the recipe starting at step 7 to complete the granita. If desired, mix in 1–2 tablespoons Pernod, anisette, or dark rum after freezing for about 2 hours. Serve within 24 hours.

## Pink Grapefruit Granita

Pink grapefruit, especially Texas Ruby Reds with their bright pink pulp, make a prettier granita than their paler relatives.

Make a grapefruit syrup: In a small saucepan, stir together ¾ cup (6 oz/185 g) granulated sugar, ¾ cup (6 fl oz/180 ml) water, and 2 teaspoons grated grapefruit zest. Place over medium-high heat and bring to a steady boil. Boil, stirring frequently, until the syrup is clear with no visible grains of sugar, 1–2 minutes. Remove from the heat, pour into a heatproof bowl, and let cool to room temperature, about 20 minutes. Cover and refrigerate until the syrup is very cold, about 1 hour.

If desired, pour the chilled syrup through a fine-mesh sieve into a bowl to strain out the zest. Press hard on the zest with the back of a spoon to extract as much flavor as possible. If you prefer a bright pink granita, stir in 2 teaspoons grenadine syrup. Add 1½ cups (12 fl oz/375 ml) unsweetened grapefruit juice to the cold syrup and stir well.

Proceed with the recipe starting at step 7 to complete the granita. If desired, mix in 1–2 tablespoons crème de cassis, anisette, or light rum after freezing for about 2 hours. Serve within 24 hours.

## Pomegranate Granita

If the pomegranate juice is concentrated, reconstitute it before making the granita. Some brands are more tart than others, so taste the juice before making the granita and add an extra tablespoon or two of sugar if necessary.

Make a pomegranate syrup: In a bowl, whisk together 3 cups (24 fl oz/750 ml) room-temperature pomegranate juice, about ¾ cup (6 oz/185 g) granulated sugar (or a little more if the juice is particularly tart), and 1 tablespoon fresh lime juice until the sugar is dissolved and the mixture no longer feels or appears to be grainy, 10–15 minutes (this syrup is not heated, since the pomegranate juice would lose some of its fresh flavor). Cover and refrigerate until very cold, about 1 hour.

Proceed with the recipe starting at step 7 to complete the granita. If desired, mix in 1–2 tablespoons brandy, bourbon, or maraschino liqueur after freezing for about 2 hours. Serve within 24 hours.

## Mint Granita

Team scoops of this granita with bright red Pomegranate Granita for a delightful and decorative holiday dessert.

Make a mint syrup: In a small saucepan, stir together 1¼ cups (10 oz/315 g) granulated sugar and 1 cup (8 fl oz/250 ml) water. Stir in the leaves from 1 bunch mint (about 1 cup/1 oz/30 g packed leaves). Push the leaves down into the liquid to submerge them. Place over medium-high heat and bring to a steady boil. Boil, stirring frequently, until the syrup is clear with no visible grains of sugar, 1–2 minutes. Remove from the heat, pour into a heatproof bowl, and let cool to room temperature, about 20 minutes. Cover and refrigerate until the syrup is very cold, about 1 hour. Leave the mint in the syrup while cooling.

Pour the syrup through a fine-mesh sieve into a bowl. Press hard on the mint leaves to extract as much liquid and flavor as possible. Stir in 1 tablespoon fresh lemon juice.

Proceed with the recipe starting at step 7 to complete the granita. For additional mint flavor and intense green color, mix in 2 tablespoons green crème de menthe after freezing for about 2 hours. Serve within 24 hours.

## Espresso Granita

Be sure to start with good, fresh espresso-roast or other dark-roast coffee beans, and brew to double strength if using regular coffee beans, since freezing diminishes the potency.

Pour 3 cups (24 fl oz/750 ml) freshly brewed, very hot espresso or double-strength coffee into a heatproof bowl. Add ¾ cup (6 oz/185 g) granulated sugar and stir until the sugar is completely dissolved, 3–5 minutes. Let cool to room temperature, about 20 minutes. Cover and refrigerate until the syrup is very cold, about 1 hour.

Proceed with the recipe starting at step 7 to complete the granita. If desired, mix in ¼ cup (2 fl oz/60 ml) Kahlúa or other coffee liqueur or chocolate liqueur, after freezing for about 2 hours. Serve within 24 hours.

### PASTRY CHEF'S TIP

*When serving granita to kids, scoop it into paper cups for homemade snow cones. They will be a hit, especially in the hot summer months. (Remember to omit the liqueur from the recipe.)*

## Spiced Cider Granita

Serve this as a light dessert during the fall months, along with some Tuile Cookies (page 22). It's also good accompanied by oatmeal raisin cookies or gingersnaps.

Make a spiced cider syrup: In a small saucepan, stir together ½ cup (4 oz/125 g) granulated sugar and 2½ cups (20 fl oz/625 ml) apple or pear cider. Place 1 cinnamon stick, broken in half, 4 whole cloves, and 4 whole allspice on a small piece of cheesecloth (muslin) and tie securely with kitchen string to form a small bundle; add to the pan. Place the pan over medium-high heat and bring to a steady boil. Boil, stirring frequently, until the syrup is clear with no visible grains of sugar, 1–2 minutes. Remove from the heat, pour into a heatproof bowl, and let cool to room temperature, about 20 minutes. Cover and refrigerate until the syrup is very cold, about 1 hour. Leave the spice bundle in the cider syrup while cooling.

Remove and discard the spice bundle, then stir in 1 tablespoon fresh lemon juice. Proceed with the recipe starting at step 7 to complete the granita. If desired, mix in ¼ cup (2 fl oz/60 ml) hard cider, Calvados or other apple brandy, or Cognac after freezing for about 2 hours. Serve within 24 hours.

# 5

# Composed Frozen Desserts

Now that you know how to put together a variety of
sauces, ice creams, and sorbets, you are ready to combine
their flavors and textures to make such composed frozen
desserts as a multilayered ice cream torte and single-serving
baked Alaskas. Here, you'll also learn how to prepare
choux pastry for profiteroles and a different type of custard,
a curd, for an airy frozen soufflé.

# Frozen Key Lime Soufflé

The tart juice and zest of Key limes—small, round fruits from southern Florida—make brightly flavored *curd*, a type of custard. Lightened with whipped cream and frozen, the lime curd is transformed into an airy cold dessert, similar in texture but easier to make than a baked soufflé.

## 1 Separate the eggs

If you need help separating eggs, turn to page 34. Have ready 2 small bowls and 1 larger heatproof glass or stainless-steel bowl. Holding an egg in your hand, strike it sharply on its equator on the work surface, cracking it, then hold it upright over 1 small bowl and lift away the top half of the shell. The yolk should be resting in the bottom half. Working gently so as not to break the yolk, transfer the yolk back and forth between the shell halves over the bowl, allowing all the egg white to drop into the bowl. Drop the yolk into the heatproof bowl and transfer the white to the remaining small bowl. Repeat with 2 more eggs.

## 2 Zest and juice the limes and mix the ingredients

For more details on zesting and juicing citrus, turn to page 40. Use a rasp grater to grate 1 tablespoon of the lime zest and set aside. To juice the limes, cut each in half crosswise and use a citrus reamer to squeeze ½ cup (4 fl oz/125 ml) juice into a bowl. Strain the juice and set aside. Crack the remaining 3 eggs into a 3-quart (3-l) nonreactive saucepan and add the egg yolks. Whisk until the yolks are broken up and the mixture is thickened. Add the sugar, lime zest, lime juice, and salt to the egg yolks. Whisk all around the sides and the bottom of the pan until well blended. Scatter the butter pieces over the liquid in the saucepan.

## 3 Cook the lime curd

Place the saucepan over medium heat. Whisk constantly until the mixture is warm, the butter is melted, and the sugar has dissolved. Spoon a small amount onto a plate, let cool, and then touch to test for graininess. Now, switch to a wooden spoon and stir constantly, including the bottom and the sides of the pan, to prevent scorching. After 5 to 7 minutes, the custard will begin to thicken. Continue to stir constantly until a few thick bubbles pop at the pan edges and the curd thickly coats the spoon so that a finger drawn through it leaves a trail. As soon as thick bubbles appear, remove from the heat. ›

6 large eggs

8–10 Key limes, plus 1 or 2 for garnish

1¼ cups (10 oz/315 g) granulated sugar

⅛ teaspoon salt

4 tablespoons (2 oz/60 g) unsalted butter, cut into 12 equal pieces

1 cup (8 fl oz/250 ml) cold heavy (double) cream

Citrus leaves for garnish, optional

MAKES ABOUT 8 SERVINGS

### CHEF'S TIP

*Key limes are small, yellowish limes from the Florida Keys that make a brief showing in the markets in late spring and early summer. If you can't find them, use Persian limes, which are more readily available.*

4>>

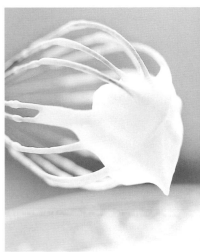

4 **Cool the lime curd**
Immediately after removing the pan from the heat, use a rubber spatula to scrape the curd into a medium heatproof glass or stainless-steel bowl. If there are any browned or scorched flecks on the bottom of the pan, leave them behind. Fill a large bowl halfway with ice cubes and enough cold water just to cover the cubes. Nestle the bowl with the curd into the ice cubes and let stand, stirring gently every 5 minutes or so, until the curd is cooled to room temperature, 15–20 minutes. As the ice melts, be sure the water level does not rise high enough to flow into the curd.

5 **Refrigerate the lime curd**
After the lime curd has cooled, remove the medium bowl from the bowl of ice cubes. Place a piece of plastic wrap directly onto the surface of the curd, which will prevent a coating, or a "skin," from forming as the curd chills. Refrigerate the curd until it is well chilled, at least 3 hours. (You can also make the curd in advance and refrigerate it for up to 24 hours before making the soufflé.)

6 **Whip the cream**
Pour the cold cream into a chilled bowl (cold cream whips faster and will achieve a greater volume than cream that is room temperature). Using a handheld mixer or stand mixer fitted with the whip attachment, beat the cream on medium-low speed until thickened and little ridges are left on the surface of the cream when the whip is moved. Increase the speed slowly to medium-high while continuing to beat, moving the whip around the bowl if using a handheld mixer so that the cream is evenly mixed. Beat until the cream just begins to hold a peak when the whip is lifted, 2 to 3 minutes. Continue to beat until the cream stays firmly upright with a slight droop when the whip is lifted, 1–2 minutes longer. These are called *soft peaks*. Watch carefully to avoid overbeating, which will cause the cream to clump or look grainy. For more details on whipping cream, turn to page 30. ❯

**PASTRY CHEF'S TIP**
*The base of this dessert is lime curd, a thick, creamy mixture made from lime juice, eggs, sugar, and butter. It also makes a wonderful filling for a tart or a sweet spread for toast or biscuits. Or, you can add the whipped cream to the lime curd, and use the mixture to fill tuile cookie cups (page 22).*

## 7 Mix the soufflé

Have ready a 1- to 1½-quart (1- to 1½-l) soufflé dish or freezerproof serving bowl. Next, use a rubber spatula to transfer about ½ cup (4 fl oz/125 ml) of the whipped cream into the lime curd, then gently stir it in to lighten the curd. This will also help the soufflé stay airy. Now, dollop the remaining whipped cream on top of the curd and use the spatula and sweeping over-and-under motions to blend together the whipped cream and the curd until no streaks of white remain. This technique is called *folding*. Be sure to reach all the way down to the bottom of the bowl to incorporate the whipped cream evenly but lightly throughout the curd.

### MAKE-AHEAD TIP

*You can freeze lime curd in a tightly covered container for up to 1 month. Because the curd has a dense texture with a low moisture content, there is no need to thaw it. When ready to use, spoon out exactly what you need and thaw before use.*

## 8 Freeze the soufflé

Gently, so as not to deflate the mixture, use the spatula to transfer the mixture to the soufflé dish. Use the spatula to gently form attractive swirls on top. Cover the soufflé with plastic wrap and place in the freezer until frozen, at least 3 hours or up to 24 hours.

## 9 Serve the soufflé

About 1½ hours before serving the soufflé, remove from the freezer and place in the refrigerator to thaw slightly, for the best flavor and texture. When served, the soufflé should be firm but not frozen solid. When ready to serve, cut 1 or 2 Key limes into thin slices. Garnish the soufflé with the lime slices and citrus leaves.

# Finishing touches

*You can vary a frozen soufflé with one of these three simple ideas: Make individual soufflés in single-serving ramekins garnished with one thin lime slice and serve the ramekins on a decorative platter. Persian limes can be used as individual serving "dishes" by simply cutting off the top and hollowing out the lime. Or, to add color and a bit of flavor, sprinkle grated lime zest onto the center of the soufflé.*

### Individual frozen soufflés (top left)
Evenly divide the soufflé mixture among eight ½-cup (4–fl oz/125-ml) individual soufflé dishes and freeze as directed. Remove the soufflés from the freezer 1 hour before serving. Garnish with thin lime slices and citrus leaves.

### Frozen soufflés in lime cups (left)
Select 8 large Persian limes. Cut off the stem end of each lime to create a cap. Using a spoon, hollow out the lime, removing the flesh. Fill with the soufflé mixture, then freeze. Place on a citrus leaf to serve.

### Frozen soufflé garnished with zest (above)
Grate lime zest with a rasp grater (page 40) and top the souffle with a small mound of the zest.

# Profiteroles

These small, flaky pastries are made from a simple dough of flour, eggs, butter, and water known as *choux* pastry. When the dough is shaped, it puffs up dramatically in the oven to form a crisp golden crust and hollow interior, a perfect receptacle for a scoop of ice cream and a pool of warm chocolate sauce.

## 1 Prepare the baking sheet and oven

Position a rack in the center of the oven and preheat it to 400°F (200°C). Put a small amount of butter on a piece of waxed paper and lightly coat an 11-by-15-by-1-inch (25-by-38-by-2.5-cm) shiny metal rimmed baking sheet. (Profiteroles tend to burn if baked on dark baking sheets.)

## 2 Make the pastry

Put the butter, water, and salt in a 2- or 3-quart (2- or 3-l) saucepan. Place the pan over medium-high heat and cook, stirring occasionally with a wooden spoon, until the mixture comes to a full boil, with bubbles breaking over the entire surface, 3–5 minutes. Remove the pan from the heat and immediately add the flour all at once. Beat the mixture vigorously with the wooden spoon, incorporating all of the flour into a smooth batter. Reduce the heat to medium and return the pan to the heat. Now, continue to cook and stir constantly until the batter thickens and forms a mass or ball that comes away cleanly from the sides of the pan but leaves a thin film of batter on the bottom during stirring. At this point, steam should no longer be rising from the batter, which indicates that all of the excess moisture has evaporated. This will take 4–5 minutes of vigorous beating. When the batter reaches this stage, immediately remove the pan from the heat.

## 3 Beat in the eggs

Let the mixture cool in the pan for 5 minutes. Meanwhile, crack the eggs into a small bowl. While beating the batter with the wooden spoon with one hand, pour 1 of the eggs into the saucepan with your other hand. (Don't be concerned about being exact here. Just make sure 1 egg yolk drops into the pan, and "eyeball" the amount that would equal 1 egg white.) Continue to beat until the egg is fully incorporated and the dough is smooth, a little shiny, and a bit more golden. Add the second egg, beating in the same way. Now add the remaining 2 eggs, one at a time, beating in the same way after each addition. After all 4 eggs have been added, the batter should be smooth, golden, shiny, and somewhat sticky.

For the choux pastry

Unsalted butter for coating the baking sheet

½ cup (4 oz/125 g) unsalted butter, cut into 12 equal pieces

1 cup (8 fl oz/250 ml) water

¼ teaspoon salt

1 cup (5 oz/ 155 g) all-purpose (plain) flour

4 large eggs, at room temperature

For the filling and sauce

1 batch French Vanilla Ice Cream (page 47) or other ice cream or gelato of your choice

3 tablespoons confectioners' (icing) sugar

1½–2 cups (12–16 fl oz/375–500 ml) Chocolate Sauce (page 24)

MAKES 4 SERVINGS

**PASTRY CHEF'S TIP**

*If you don't have a large baking sheet, use 2 smaller sheets and bake them side by side or on the upper and lower racks of the oven. Rotate the placement of the baking sheets halfway through the baking time. Or, use 1 baking sheet and bake in 2 batches, keeping the remaining batter in the saucepan, tightly covered, so that it stays warm.*

*Keep the base and top of each pastry near each other. That way, when reassembled with the ice cream in the middle, the desserts will have a finished look.*

### 4 Shape the pastries

For more details on how to use a pastry bag, turn to page 39. Fit a 12–14 inch (30–35 cm) pastry bag with a 1-inch tip and fill the bag with the dough. Pipe the dough into 1 inch (2.5 cm) mounds on the baking sheet leaving 2 inches (5 cm) of space between each mound. (Alternatively, use a tablespoon to scoop out heaping tablespoonfuls of batter.) Resist the urge to go back and add batter to a mound to make it even with the others; the added batter won't puff up as part of the original mound. Now wet your fingertip with water and gently push down any peaks on the dough mounds; you don't want to flatten the mounds, but you do want to try to make the surface as smooth as possible.

### 5 Bake the pastries

Place the baking sheet in the oven. Bake the pastries for 15 minutes, then, without opening the oven, reduce the heat to 375°F (190°C). It is important not to open the oven door during the first half of baking or the profiteroles may collapse. Continue baking until the pastries are well puffed, dry on the outside, and a rich golden brown, 8–12 minutes more. Try not to underbake them, or the profiteroles will be soggy and not as flavorful. Remove the baking sheet from the oven and turn the oven off.

### 6 Dry the pastries

As soon as you remove the baking sheet from the oven, use the tip of a small knife to make 2 tiny punctures in the top of each pastry. This will allow the steam to escape and the interior of the puffs to dry out a bit. Now, return the baking sheet to the turned-off oven. Let the pastries dry in the oven for 5 minutes. Remove the baking sheet from the oven and transfer the pastries to a wire rack to cool completely for at least 30 minutes. (If you are not serving the profiteroles immediately, they can be stored in a single layer in a tightly covered plastic container at room temperature for 24 hours or in the freezer for up to 2 weeks. They will lose their crispness in the freezer, but this can be repaired by placing the thawed pastries in a single layer on a baking sheet and heating in a preheated 300°F/150°C oven until they again feel crisp and dry, 8–10 minutes.)

### 7 Cut off the pastry tops

Use a serrated knife and a gentle sawing motion to cut off the top of each profiterole, cutting about halfway between the center and the top. Use your fingers or a small fork to gently pull out and discard any soft, yellow undercooked batter from inside the tops and bases. Be sure to keep the top and base of each profiterole next to each other, so that you can put each top on its corresponding base when it is time to reassemble the profiteroles. ›

### 8 Fill the pastry

Dip a small ice cream scoop into hot water and warm briefly. Pull the scoop across the ice cream to form a rounded scoop. Release the scoop onto 1 profiterole base. For more details on scooping ice cream, turn to page 42. Repeat to fill the remaining profiteroles with ice cream. Profiteroles are best filled with ice cream or gelato rather than sorbet or granita; the latter are too watery and will render the pastry soggy within a few minutes. Replace the tops of the profiteroles. The ice cream should be visible but not hanging over the sides. Put the confectioners' sugar in a small fine-mesh sieve and gently tap the sieve while holding it over the profiteroles to dust them lightly with the sugar.

### 9 Serve the profiteroles

Put the chocolate sauce in a small saucepan over very low heat. Stirring often, warm the sauce until it is a pourable consistency. (The sauce can also be reheated in a microwave oven. Heat for 10–20 seconds, then stir. Repeat if necessary, watching carefully so that the sauce doesn't burn.) Spoon about 3 tablespoons of the warmed chocolate sauce onto each of 4 dessert plates, spreading it with the back of a spoon to cover the bottom of the plate. Set 3 profiteroles atop the sauce. Serve right away.

**MAKE-AHEAD TIP**

*You can make the pastries up to 1 month in advance and freeze them in the freezer. Let them cool completely, then wrap tightly in plastic wrap and then in aluminum foil. Thaw at room temperature before filling with ice cream and serve right away.*

## Serving ideas

*Other ice cream flavors, such as mint–chocolate chip, can be used to fill profiteroles, and the sauce can be drizzled on top of the puffs instead of pooled underneath. For a spectacular dessert, serve a trio of pastries, each filled with a different ice cream and accompanied by a different topping. Or, fill éclairs with ice cream instead of pastry cream, for an interesting variation on a familiar bakery staple.*

**Mint–chocolate chip profiteroles** (top left)
Fill the baked pastries with Mint–Chocolate Chip Ice Cream (page 62) and top with room temperature Chocolate Sauce (page 24).

**Trio of profiteroles** (left)
Here, French Vanilla Ice Cream (page 47) is paired with Caramel Sauce (page 26), Espresso Ice Cream (page 52) with Chocolate Sauce (page 24), and Strawberry Ice Cream (page 54) with Sweetened Whipped Cream (page 30).

**Ice cream éclairs** (above)
Pipe strips of the choux pastry 3–4 inches (7.5–10 cm) long and 1 inch (2.5 cm) wide. Bake as directed, then fill with two scoops of ice cream.

# Individual Baked Alaskas

Putting ice cream into a hot oven sounds daring, and only adds to the allure of this special-occasion dessert. The contrast of textures, temperatures, and flavors—airy, slightly charred sweet meringue; cold, creamy ice cream; a rich cake base—is the main appeal of this showy classic.

## 1 Slice the pound cake and cut into rounds

Line a rimmed baking sheet with parchment (baking) paper. If the parchment won't lie flat, "glue" it to the baking sheet with small dabs of butter placed under the sheet at each corner. Using a serrated knife, cut 4 slices, each about 1 inch (2.5 cm) thick, from the pound cake. Reserve the remaining cake for another use. (You can drizzle it with Chocolate Sauce (page 24) or serve it alongside scoops of your favorite ice cream.) Using a 3-inch (7.5-cm) round pastry cutter, cut a circle from each cake slice, pressing down and lifting straight up to make a perfect circle. Arrange the pound cake circles on the prepared baking sheet, leaving at least 3 inches (7.5 cm) between the slices.

## 2 Brush the pound cake with liqueur

Pour the liqueur or syrup into a small dish. Then use a small pastry brush to lightly brush the top of each cake circle with the liquid. This will moisten the pound cake and intensify the raspberry flavor. Place the baking sheet in the freezer and freeze until the cake circles are firm, about 15 minutes.

## 3 Prepare the ice cream

Dip an ice cream scoop into hot water and warm briefly. The scoop should be the same diameter as the pound cake circles. Pull the scoop across the ice cream to form a rounded scoop. Release the scoop onto the pound cake circle. Repeat with the remaining ice cream and pound cake circles. Place the baking sheet in the coldest part of the freezer until the ice cream is very firm, about 1 hour. If the ice cream gets too firm, it will hinder applying the meringue. If you are not planning to finish the desserts right away, cover the baking sheet with aluminum foil and return to the freezer for up to 24 hours before continuing.

1 purchased pound cake, 9-by-5-inch (23-by-13-cm)

2 tablespoons raspberry eau-de-vie, raspberry liqueur, or raspberry syrup

1 pt (16 fl oz/500 ml) Raspberry Ice Cream (page 57)

4 large eggs

¼ teaspoon cream of tartar

½ cup (4 oz/125 g) granulated sugar

MAKES 4 SERVINGS

### PASTRY CHEF'S TIP

*Baked Alaskas can be made with other bases, such as sponge cake or cakelike brownies. Don't use dense brownies; they will freeze too hard and will be difficult to cut with a fork when served.*

4

5

4 **Separate the eggs**

Up to 1 hour before baking, separate the eggs to make the meringue. If you need help separating eggs, turn to page 34. Have ready 2 small bowls and 1 larger glass or stainless steel bowl. Holding an egg in your hand, strike it sharply on its equator on the work surface, cracking it, then hold it upright over 1 small bowl and lift away the top half of the shell. The yolk should be resting in the bottom half. Working gently so as not to break the yolk, transfer the yolk back and forth between the shell halves over the bowl, allowing all the egg white to drop into the bowl. Drop the yolk into the second small bowl and transfer the white to the large bowl. Repeat with the remaining 3 eggs. Reserve the yolks for another use.

5 **Beat the egg whites with the cream of tartar**

Fit a mixer with the whip attachment and beat the egg white mixture with the 2 tablespoons sugar on medium speed until foamy, about 1 minute. Sprinkle the cream of tartar into the egg whites and continue beating for a few seconds.

6 **Beat the meringue**

Increase the mixer speed to medium and beat until the egg whites begin to thicken, 2–3 minutes. Increase the mixer speed to medium-high and beat until the egg whites fall in soft mounds when a rubber spatula is gently run through them. Increase the mixer speed to high and sprinkle in the sugar, 1 tablespoon at a time, beating the egg whites for about 15 seconds after each addition. The egg whites will begin to mound higher and stand up in softly drooping peaks when a rubber spatula is run through them. When all of the sugar has been added, continue to beat until the egg whites form *stiff peaks* with tips that barely droop when the whip is raised, 1 minute. Once they reach this stage, stop beating.

7 **Coat the ice cream with meringue**

Take the baking sheet from the freezer. Working quickly, use a thin offset spatula to cover all of the ice cream–topped cake rounds completely with the meringue. The meringue will insulate the ice cream when it is in the oven. >

**PASTRY CHEF'S TIP**

*If you own a copper bowl, you can use it to whip egg whites without the addition of cream of tartar. The copper reacts chemically with the egg protein to produce tall, fluffy, stable whites with a satiny finish.*

## 8 Create swirls in the meringue

Use the spatula to make little swirls and points in the meringue. The edges of these textured areas will brown in the oven. Return the baking sheet, uncovered, to the freezer for at least 10 minutes or up to 1 hour.

**CHEF'S TIP**

*If you have forgotten how many eggs you have separated, you can weigh the yolks or the whites. A single large yolk weighs ¾ ounce (20 g) and 1 large white weighs 1¼ ounces (37 g). Divide the total weight by the weight of a single yolk or white to arrive at the exact number of eggs.*

## 9 Bake the baked Alaskas

Position a rack in the center of the oven and preheat the oven to 450°F (230°C). The high oven heat will help brown the meringue quickly so that the ice cream center remains frozen. Let the oven heat for at least 10 minutes. Turn on the oven light. When the oven is hot, take the baking sheet directly from the freezer and place it in the preheated oven. Bake until the meringue is pale golden and the tips of the swirls are browned, 4 to 5 minutes. While baking, watch carefully through the oven door, but don't open the oven door or the heat will escape.

## 10 Serve the baked Alaskas

When the baked Alaskas are done, slide a wide offset spatula under each dessert and transfer to an individual plate. Serve them right away while the meringue is still warm and the ice cream is still cold.

# Finishing touches

*Baked Alaska is delicious on its own, but you can also serve the dessert with a complementary fruit sauce, such as a berry purée. Or, make a single large baked Alaska with an ice cream that has a bold color and full flavor. For example, vanilla ice cream will not provide much contrast to the meringue, but chocolate, berry, pumpkin, or caramel will. Another idea is to sprinkle the meringue with flaked coconut before baking it.*

**Baked Alaska with raspberry purée** (top left)
In a blender, process 4 cups (1 lb/500 g) raspberries and 3 tablespoons confectioners' (icing) sugar until smooth. Strain through a fine-mesh sieve.

**Large caramel baked Alaska** (left)
Use a 9-inch (23-cm) round cake pan that is 1–1½ inches (2.5–4 cm) high. Mound with 1 batch Caramel Ice Cream (page 53), and freeze as directed. Cover with a meringue made of 6 large egg whites, ¼ teaspoon cream of tartar, and ¾ cup (6 oz/185 g) granulated sugar. Bake for 4 to 5 minutes.

**Baked Alaska with toasted coconut** (above)
Sprinkle each individual baked Alaska with 1 tablespoon flaked dried coconut before baking.

## Tiramisu Ice Cream Torte

All the flavors of tiramisu—thick, rich mascarpone cheese, robust espresso, dark chocolate, delicate ladyfingers, and sweet Marsala—are present in this elegant two-toned torte. But here, the mascarpone and espresso are churned into ice creams to create a frozen variation on the Italian classic.

48–56 purchased sponge-cake ladyfingers, 7–8 oz (220–250 g) total

⅓ cup (3 fl oz/80 ml) Marsala

1 batch Espresso Ice Cream (page 52)

⅓ cup (3 fl oz/80 ml) Chocolate Sauce (page 24), warmed

1 batch Mascarpone Ice Cream (page 53)

2–3 teaspoons unsweetened regular or Dutch-process cocoa powder

10–12 chocolate-covered coffee beans, optional

MAKES 10–12 SERVINGS

**PASTRY CHEF'S TIP**
*You can use a microwave oven to soften ice cream for molding into desserts. But be careful, or you will melt the outside while the center remains frozen. Microwave the ice cream in 10-second intervals, and stir gently after each interval to preserve its texture.*

1 **Line the pan with plastic wrap**
Tear off a piece of plastic wrap at least 30 inches (75 cm) long. Place the center of the piece of plastic wrap in the center of a 9-inch (23-cm) springform pan. Press the wrap into the pan to line the bottom and sides, leaving at least 6 inches (15 cm) of plastic wrap overhanging the edges. Now repeat this process with a second piece of plastic wrap, arranging the second piece perpendicular to the first, thus creating an overhang on all sides. (This will later be folded up and over the torte.)

2 **Arrange the ladyfingers in the pan**
Open the package of ladyfingers. They will likely be attached side by side. If so, leave them attached. (Some of the ladyfingers will be used to line the sides of the pan, and they will be easier to arrange if attached.) Arrange enough ladyfingers around the sides of the pan, standing them upright and placing them side by side with rounded sides facing out, to fit snugly around the circumference of the pan like a picket fence. Cover the bottom of the pan snugly with the remaining ladyfingers, rounded side down. If necessary, trim some of the ladyfingers to make a snug fit on the bottom of the pan. The entire pan, bottom and sides, should now be lined with ladyfingers.

3 **Soak the ladyfingers**
Pour the Marsala into a small dish. Using a medium-sized pastry brush (about 2 inches/5 cm wide), dip the brush into the Marsala and brush the ladyfingers, soaking them evenly and generously with the wine. Place the pan in the refrigerator for 15–30 minutes to allow the ladyfingers to firm slightly; this will make it easier to spread the ice cream over them.

4 **Soften the espresso ice cream**
While the ladyfingers are chilling, remove the espresso ice cream from the freezer and let it stand in the refrigerator for about 30 minutes or at room temperature for about 15 minutes, stirring once or twice so that it softens evenly to a thick, spreadable consistency. The ice cream should not melt, however. If it gets too soft, put it back into the freezer for a few minutes. >

## 5 Spread the ice cream into the pan

Using a rubber spatula or a spoon, drop the Espresso Ice Cream in dollops evenly over the bottom of the ladyfinger-lined springform pan. Use a small offset spatula to spread the ice cream evenly over the ladyfingers, taking care not to dislodge them. The pan will be about half full. Cover the pan with aluminum foil, put the pan in the freezer, and freeze until the ice cream has hardened again, at least 30 minutes.

## 6 Spread the sauce on the ice cream

Using the spoon or rubber spatula, carefully spread the warm chocolate sauce over the espresso ice cream to cover it completely with a thin layer (warm sauce is easier to spread). Cover the pan with foil and return it to the freezer until the chocolate sauce is firm, at least 15 minutes. Leave the warm chocolate sauce out.

## 7 Soften and spread the mascarpone ice cream

Remove the mascarpone ice cream from the freezer and soften it in the same way as you did the espresso ice cream in step 4. Spread the mascarpone ice cream on top of the layer of chocolate sauce, again using an offset spatula as you did in step 5. Cover the pan with foil again and freeze until the ice cream is firm, at least 3 hours or up to 24 hours.

## 8 Garnish the torte

When you are ready to serve the torte, unlatch and remove the sides of the springform pan. Unwrap the torte; remove the bottom of the springform pan and peel away all of the plastic wrap. Place the torte on a serving platter. Put the cocoa powder in a small fine-mesh sieve and gently tap the sieve while holding it over the torte, dusting it lightly and evenly with the powder. Mark the center of the torte with a toothpick, and then use a heavy knife to score the top of the torte into 10–12 even wedges. Press a chocolate-covered coffee bean, if using, into each wedge.

## 9 Slice and serve the torte

For the prettiest wedges that clearly show all the layers of the torte, use the heavy knife to cut straight down from the toothpick to the edge along the scored lines. Dip the knife in hot water after each cut. For more details on slicing frozen tortes, turn to page 43. For the best flavor, let the wedges stand for 2 to 3 minutes before serving to allow the ice cream to soften slightly.

**PASTRY CHEF'S TIP**

*If you use crisp Italian ladyfingers, instead of the common sponge-cake type, increase the Marsala to ½ cup (4 fl oz/125 ml). The cookies will absorb the Marsala but still remain firm. As the torte chills, the ladyfingers will soften.*

# Ice Cream Torte Variations

Once you have perfected Tiramisu Ice Cream Torte (page 118), you will have the knowledge and confidence to create other frozen tortes. You can make them with nearly any ice cream, gelato, or sorbet, but don't try to use a granita, as it will melt too quickly. Most sorbets, because they don't contain fat, also melt more quickly than ice cream, so if you are using a sorbet in a torte, serve the torte immediately after cutting it into wedges. If you are using both a sorbet and an ice cream or gelato, make the sorbet the bottom layer, which tends to stay colder. Each variation makes 10 to 12 servings.

## Chocolate-Orange Ice Cream Torte

Substitute 2 tablespoons thawed frozen orange juice concentrate mixed with 2 tablespoons water for the Grand Marnier, if desired.

Line a 9-inch (23-cm) springform pan with 2 pieces of plastic wrap, leaving at least a 6-inch (15-cm) overhang on all sides. Arrange 48–56 sponge-cake ladyfingers over the bottom and up the sides of the pan. Brush the ladyfingers with ⅓ cup (3 fl oz/80 ml) Grand Marnier.

Soften 1 batch Orange Sorbet (page 86) and spread over the ladyfingers. Cover with aluminum foil and freeze until firm, about 30 minutes. Next, warm ⅓ cup (3 fl oz/80 ml) Chocolate Sauce (page 24) and spread over the sorbet. Re-cover and freeze until firm, about 15 minutes. Finally, soften 1 batch French Vanilla Ice Cream (page 47) and spread over the chocolate sauce. Re-cover and freeze for 3–24 hours.

When ready to serve, garnish with 2–3 tablespoons grated bittersweet or semisweet (plain) chocolate (page 37). Have ready 10–12 thin orange slices, and press 1 slice into the top of each serving wedge. Cut into slices and serve.

## White Chocolate–Raspberry Ice Cream Torte

If desired, replace the framboise with a high-quality raspberry syrup.

Line a 9-inch (23-cm) springform pan with 2 pieces of plastic wrap, leaving at least a 6-inch (15-cm) overhang on all sides. Arrange 48–56 sponge cake ladyfingers over the bottom and up the sides of the pan. Brush the ladyfingers with ⅓ cup (3 fl oz/80 ml) framboise.

Soften 1 batch Raspberry Sorbet (page 87) and spread it evenly over the ladyfingers. Cover with aluminum foil and freeze until firm, about 30 minutes. Next, in a bowl, stir together ⅓ cup (3 oz/90 g) high-quality seedless raspberry preserves and 1 tablespoon framboise. Spread the mixture evenly over the raspberry sorbet. Re-cover and freeze until firm, about 15 minutes. Finally, soften 1 batch White Chocolate Gelato (page 74) and spread it evenly over the preserves. Re-cover and freeze for 3–24 hours.

When ready to serve, arrange 1 cup (4 oz/125 g) raspberries around the edge of the torte. Cut into slices and serve.

## Strawberry-Banana Ice Cream Torte

For kids, omit the liqueur and use a clear flavored syrup such as vanilla or almond.

Line a 9-inch (23-cm) springform pan with 2 pieces of plastic wrap, leaving at least a 6-inch (15-cm) overhang on all sides. Arrange 48–56 sponge-cake ladyfingers over the bottom and up the sides of the pan. Brush the ladyfingers with ⅓ cup (3 fl oz/80 ml) banana liqueur or light rum.

Soften 1 batch Banana Ice Cream (page 57) and spread it evenly over the ladyfingers. Cover with aluminum foil and freeze until firm, about 30 minutes. Next, warm ⅓ cup (3 fl oz/80 ml) Chocolate Sauce (page 24) and spread it evenly over the banana ice cream. Re-cover and freeze until firm, about 15 minutes. Finally, soften 1 batch Strawberry Ice Cream (page 54) and spread it evenly over the chocolate sauce. Re-cover and freeze for 3–24 hours.

When ready to serve, arrange 2 cups (8 oz/250 g) hulled small whole strawberries, hulled side down, around the edge of the torte. Peel 2 firm yellow bananas and slice ¼ inch (6 mm) thick, then arrange in a concentric circle inside the strawberry circle. Cut into slices and serve.

# Ice Cream Sandwiches

When you make your own ice cream sandwiches, you can match the ice cream flavor and cookie with the season. Here, pale gold pumpkin ice cream laced with spices is sandwiched between equally spicy gingersnaps and then rolled in crunchy toasted nuts to yield an ideal autumn treat.

## 1 Toast the pecans

Position a rack in the middle of the oven and preheat to 350°F (180°C). Pour the nuts onto a small rimmed baking sheet. Place the baking sheet in the oven and toast the nuts for about 3 minutes. Remove the baking sheet from the oven and use a wooden spoon to stir the nuts so that the ones that were in the center are now at the edges. Return the pan to the oven and continue toasting, stirring occasionally, until the nuts have turned a shade darker brown and smell fragrant and toasty, 3–6 minutes longer. The nuts can go from toasted to burnt very quickly, so check carefully every minute or so after the first 6 minutes. When the nuts are toasted, remove the pan from the oven and use a spoon or metal spatula to transfer the nuts to a shallow dish. Let the nuts cool.

## 2 Chop the pecans

When the nuts have cooled, pour them out onto a cutting board. Use a large chef's knife and an up-and-down motion to chop them evenly. They should be finely chopped but still recognizable as nuts. Alternatively, you can chop the nuts in a food processor, using 2-second on-and-off pulses. (Nuts chopped in a food processor, however, can easily become pulverized and may have some nut "dust" from the whirling blade. After processing, shake the nuts in a fine-mesh sieve, forcing the dust through the sieve. Discard the dust.) Put the chopped nuts in a shallow dish.

## 3 Fill the cookies with ice cream

Place 1 cookie, rounded side down, on a work surface such as a kitchen counter or a baking sheet. Dip an ice cream scoop into hot water and warm briefly; the scoop should be the same diameter as the cookies. Pull the scoop across the ice cream to form a rounded scoop. Release the scoop onto the cookie. For more details on scooping ice cream, turn to page 42. Repeat until you have topped 8 of the cookies. Place the remaining cookies, flat side down, on top of the ice cream.

## 4 Press the sandwiches together

If the ice cream is soft so that the cookies will not break when pressed, gently press the top cookies down to push the ice cream evenly to the edges of the cookies. If the cookies are too fragile for this, let the sandwiches sit at room temperature for a few minutes to allow the ice cream to soften, then use the back of a metal spoon to press the ice cream gently to the sides. >

1 cup (4 oz/125 g) pecan halves

16 flat cookies, such as gingersnaps

2 cups (16 fl oz/500 ml) Pumpkin Ice Cream (page 65)

MAKES 8 SANDWICHES

**PASTRY CHEF'S TIP**

*The size of your ice cream sandwiches can vary by using different cookies. For 6 large sandwiches, use twelve 3-inch (7.5-cm) cookies, such as chocolate graham crackers. For 12 medium sandwiches, use twenty-four 2-inch (5-cm) cookies, such as chocolate wafers. For 16 small sandwiches, use thirty-two 1½-inch (4-cm) cookies, such as chocolate–chocolate chip.*

## 5 Roll the sandwiches in the toasted pecans

As each sandwich is formed, roll the exposed ice cream around the edges of the sandwich in the chopped pecans, pressing lightly with the palm of your hand so that the pecans adhere to the ice cream. Now, quickly wrap each cookie in a small piece of plastic wrap.

## 6 Freeze the ice cream sandwiches

Place the wrapped cookies in a single layer on a baking sheet and set them in the coldest part of the freezer (usually the back or the bottom part, farthest from the door) until the ice cream is frozen solid, at least 30 minutes. The ice cream sandwiches can then be placed, still wrapped, in a freezerproof locking plastic bag and stored in the freezer for up to 24 hours.

## 7 Serve the ice cream sandwiches

Take the ice cream sandwiches out of the freezer and transfer them, in the plastic wrap, to the refrigerator to soften slightly for 5–10 minutes before serving. Unwrap the sandwiches and serve right away.

**CHEF'S TIP**

*An elegant way to serve ice cream sandwiches is to wrap each one individually in waxed paper and then tie with a ribbon.*

# Ice Cream Sandwich Variations

Making the Ice Cream Sandwiches on page 125 is quick and easy, but there are a few keys to success: keep the flat sides of the cookies facing inward, don't use too large a scoop of ice cream, and soften the ice cream just enough so that the cookies won't break when you push them into it. Now that you have learned these skills, you can try an unlimited number of ice cream–and–cookie combinations. You can also mix and match a variety of presentations and garnishes, from berries to chocolate chips to sauces. Here are a trio of ideas to get you started. Each variation makes 6 or 8 sandwiches.

## Chocolate Chip–Vanilla Ice Cream Sandwiches

Plate each sandwich in a pool of Chocolate or Caramel Sauce (pages 24 and 26) for extra richness.

Have ready sixteen 2½-inch (6-cm) chocolate chip cookies and about 3 cups (24 fl oz/75 ml) French Vanilla Ice Cream (page 47) or Philadelphia-Style Vanilla Ice Cream (page 66). Arrange half of the cookies, rounded side down, on a work surface, and place a scoop of the ice cream on top of each cookie. Top with the remaining cookies, flat side down. Wrap each sandwich with plastic wrap and freeze for at least 30 minutes.

When ready to serve, let the sandwiches sit at room temperature for 5–10 minutes before unwrapping and serving.

## Caramel Ice Cream Sandwich Sundaes

This is an elegant dessert that can be made in advance and then assembled in minutes at serving time.

Have ready twelve 3-inch (7.5-cm) Tuile Cookies (page 22) baked and shaped as flat wafers or 12 vanilla wafer cookies and about 3 cups (24 fl oz/75 ml) Caramel Ice Cream (page 53). Arrange half of the cookies, rounded side down, on a work surface, and place a scoop of the ice cream on top of each cookie. Top with the remaining cookies, flat side down. Wrap each sandwich with plastic wrap and freeze for at least 30 minutes.

Spoon 2 tablespoons room-temperature Chocolate Sauce (page 24) onto one side of each of 6 dessert plates. Now spoon 2 tablespoons room-temperature Caramel Sauce (page 26) onto the other side of the plates. It's fine if the edges of the sauce run together. Place 1 sandwich in the center of each plate. If desired, garnish the edge of each plate with a stemmed strawberry. Serve right away.

## Espresso Chip Ice Cream Sandwiches

Chocolate chips not only stud the cookies, but also are pressed onto the outside of these popular sandwiches.

Have ready sixteen 2½-inch (6-cm) chocolate chip cookies and about 3 cups (24 fl oz/75 ml) Espresso Ice Cream (page 52). Arrange half of the cookies, rounded side down, on a work surface, and place a scoop of the ice cream on top of each cookie. Top with the remaining cookies, flat side down.

Pour 1 cup (6 oz/185 g) miniature chocolate chips onto a rimmed plate. As each sandwich is formed, roll the exposed ice cream around the edges of the sandwich in the chocolate chips, pressing lightly with the palm of your hand so that the chips adhere to the ice cream. Wrap each sandwich in plastic wrap and freeze for at least 30 minutes.

When ready to serve, let the sandwiches sit at room temperature for 5–10 minutes before unwrapping and serving.

# Ice Cream Bars

Adding a tiny amount of oil to the chocolate helps it harden quickly around the ice cream, creating an appealing crisp coating. Vanilla ice cream cloaked in chocolate is a classic combination, but other ice cream flavors—such as espresso, coconut, or raspberry—would be good, too.

1 batch French Vanilla Ice Cream (page 47)

9 or 16 Popsicle sticks

20 oz (625 g) bittersweet or semisweet (plain) chocolate, chopped (page 36)

2 tablespoons canola oil

MAKES 9 LARGE OR 16 SMALL ICE CREAM BARS

1 **Press the ice cream into the pan**
Tear off a piece of plastic wrap at least 16 inches (40 cm) long and press it into an 8- or 9-inch (20- or 23-cm) square metal baking pan. Smooth the plastic wrap so that it is contoured to the bottom and sides of the pan. There will be an overhang on one side. Spoon the ice cream into the plastic wrap–lined pan and use your hands or the back of a spoon to press it evenly into the pan. If the ice cream is too hard, let it soften for a few minutes at room temperature. Fold the overhang over the ice cream. Cover the pan tightly with additional plastic wrap. Place in the freezer for 1 hour or up to 6 hours to harden the ice cream.

2 **Form the ice cream into bars**
Line a rimmed baking sheet with plastic wrap. Remove the sheet from the freezer and remove the plastic wrap. Use a knife to cut the ice cream into nine 3-inch (7.5-cm) squares or sixteen 2-inch (5-cm) squares. Now, using the plastic wrap overhang, lift the entire slab of ice cream out of the pan. Set the ice cream, still on the wrap, on a work surface. Use a metal spatula to separate the squares, and transfer them to the prepared baking sheet, spacing them at least 2 inches apart. Insert a Popsicle stick halfway into one side of each square. Cover the baking sheet with plastic wrap and return to the freezer for 1–6 hours.

3 **Make the chocolate coating**
Put the chocolate and oil in a heatproof glass or stainless-steel bowl. Set the bowl over a saucepan of simmering water. Stir gently until the chocolate is melted and smooth, 3–4 minutes. Remove the bowl from the heat and let cool, stirring occasionally, until the mixture is barely lukewarm, 15–30 minutes. For more information on melting chocolate, turn to page 36.

4 **Dip the ice cream bars**
Remove the ice cream bars from the freezer. Working quickly, use the Popsicle stick to lift up 1 square. Dip it into the chocolate until the ice cream is completely covered. Let any excess chocolate drip back into the bowl. Return the dipped bar to the baking sheet. Continue dipping the remaining bars. You are likely to have extra chocolate; save it for another use.

5 **Freeze and serve the bars**
Return the dipped bars, uncovered, to the freezer, until the ice cream and coating have both hardened, at least 30 minutes or up to 24 hours. If you leave them in the freezer for longer than 2 hours, wrap each one individually in plastic wrap after they have hardened.

# Banana Split

A banana split is a soda-fountain standard, and this recipe respects that tradition, with three ice cream flavors—vanilla, chocolate, and strawberry—each topped with a complementary sauce—chocolate, butterscotch, and strawberry respectively. Bananas and ice cream are natural partners, while the whipped cream is an extra layer of richness, the nuts deliver crunch, and the cherries add a touch of bright color.

1 **Prepare the sauces**
In a small dish, use a spoon to stir together the jam and rum or orange juice until smooth; set aside. Pour the chocolate and butterscotch sauces into separate small saucepans, place over very low heat, and heat gently until they are just warm to the touch and pourable. The sauces should not feel hot. If you have an instant-read thermometer, the mixture should register 100°–110°F (38°–43°C).

2 **Prepare the bananas**
Peel the bananas and use a paring knife to cut each in half lengthwise. If the dish you will be using is not long enough to accommodate the banana, cut the halves in half crosswise.

3 **Scoop the ice cream**
Dip an ice cream scoop in hot water to warm it, then use it to form a rounded scoop from half of the vanilla ice cream. For more details on scooping ice cream, turn to page 42. Put the scoop in the center of an elongated banana split dish, or in a large stemmed ice cream sundae dish. Follow the same procedure to add a scoop each of the Strawberry Ice Cream and Chocolate Ice Cream to either side of the vanilla ice cream. Repeat using the second dish and the remaining ice cream.

4 **Garnish the ice cream**
Lay the banana halves along either side of the ice cream scoops. Spoon the jam mixture over the Strawberry Ice Cream, the chocolate sauce over the vanilla ice cream, and the butterscotch sauce over the Chocolate Ice Cream, dividing the sauces equally between the 2 dishes. If you need help using a pastry bag, turn to page 39. Fit a pastry bag with a small fluted tip, secure it with the coupler, if needed, and fold down the top. Scoop the whipped cream into the pastry bag, unfold the bag, and twist the top, pressing the whipped cream toward the tip. Pipe a swirl of whipped cream on top of each scoop of ice cream. Alternatively, use a spoon to top each scoop with a dollop of whipped cream. Sprinkle the tops of the mounds of whipped cream with the nuts. Set a cherry, stem side up, into each dollop of cream.

5 **Serve the banana split**
Set the banana split dishes onto plates (for catching drips) and serve each with 1 or 2 long-handled spoons.

¼ cup (2½ oz/75 g) strawberry jam or pineapple jam

1 tablespoon light rum or orange juice

6 tablespoons (3 fl oz/90 ml) Chocolate Sauce (page 24)

6 tablespoons (3 fl oz/90 ml) Butterscotch Sauce (page 28)

2 small ripe but firm yellow bananas

1 cup (8 fl oz/250 ml g) French Vanilla Ice Cream (page 47)

1 cup (8 fl oz/250 ml) Strawberry Ice Cream (page 54)

1 cup (8 fl oz/250 ml) Chocolate Ice Cream (page 59)

½ cup (4 fl oz/125 ml) Sweetened Whipped Cream (page 30)

¼ cup (1 oz/30 g) chopped nuts such as walnuts, peanuts, or pistachios

6 maraschino cherries with stems

MAKES 2 LARGE BANANA SPLITS, OR 2–4 SERVINGS

**CHEF'S TIP**
*If you are new to using a pastry bag, practice piping on a piece of waxed paper before you decorate your banana split. You can also experiment with different tips. When you have finished, scrape the whipped cream back into the pastry bag so that none is wasted.*

# Using Key Tools & Equipment

Having the right tools on hand is essential for every type of cooking, and frozen desserts are no exception. All the equipment described here, with the exception of the ice cream makers, is regularly used for preparing many different kinds of dishes, both savory and sweet. Even ice cream scoops can be pressed into service for such other common kitchen activities as portioning cookie dough or cake batters for cupcakes.

### Ice Cream Makers

Ice cream makers can be inexpensive and small enough to be easily stored. A hand-crank machine takes longer but will work just fine, but today most people prefer to use electric makers. They come with a paddle attachment (also called a dasher) and an insulated canister that stays icy cold during churning. You may also be able to purchase an ice cream maker attachment for your stand mixer. The mixer's canister, as well as the canisters for some ice cream machines, must be placed in the freezer before using.

If you want to avoid the need to chill the canister in your freezer, choose an ice cream maker with a built-in freezer unit. The mixing canister is sometimes removable for freezer storage.

### Kitchen Electrics

Two additional appliances will also save you time and effort. A food processor is great for making fresh fruit purées and nut pastes and for quickly chopping nuts. A handheld mixer or stand mixer with a whip attachment can whip cream or meringues in a matter of minutes.

### Knives and Cutting Boards

Three basic knives are needed for making and serving frozen desserts. A large chef's knife, a serrated knife, and a paring knife. Be sure to keep them sharp.

A good-quality plastic or wooden cutting board cleans up easily with soap and water. Designate a cutting board for desserts only, so that it stays free of odors from garlic, onion, and the like.

### Measuring Equipment

Dry ingredients are measured in dry volume cups, which usually come in sets

with graduated sizes of ¼, ⅓, ½, and 1 cup. Sturdier stainless-steel cups are preferred over plastic ones. For greater accuracy, use a scale to measure dry ingredients. The same spoons are used for measuring both wet and dry ingredients.

Liquid measuring cups look like small pitchers with horizontal markings that indicate fluid ounces, partial cups, and at least 1 cup (8 fl oz/250 ml).

## Whisks and Spoons

You'll need two types of wire whisks: A medium-sized utility whisk with long, stiff wires is handy for mixing the ingredients for a custard base. A larger balloon whisk with fine rounded, flexible wires is good for whipping cream or egg whites.

Metal spoons are valuable for stirring cold liquids together. Wooden spoons are best for stirring hot liquids since the wood doesn't transfer heat to the handle. A spoon with holes in it, called a slotted spoon, is perfect for removing solids from liquids.

## Spatulas

You will need a rubber spatula for scraping down the sides of a food processor bowl, for scraping custards into ice cream makers, for transferring ice creams and the like into pastry bags or storage containers, and for folding whipped cream into frozen soufflé bases.

A wide, thin metal spatula simplifies the transfer of delicate cookies to a cooling rack. Flexible, narrow offset metal spatulas are good for smoothing layered desserts or spreading meringue.

## Bowls and Molds

Heatproof glass is an excellent choice for all-purpose mixing bowls. Stainless-steel bowls, which are sturdy and stand up well to extreme heat and cold, are also practical. Unlined copper bowls are ideal for beating egg whites, as copper reacts with the protein in the whites to increase the volume. Do not use them (or unlined aluminum) for acidic ingredients such as citrus juices, however, as they will impart an off flavor. Small glass or metal bowls or ramekins are ideal for holding your *mise en place,* while the ramekins and a large soufflé dish are used for making frozen soufflés.

## Strainers

Colanders are handy for straining large quantities of thick mixtures, such as fruit purées. Fine-mesh sieves in a variety of sizes perform various tasks, from sifting dry ingredients such as cocoa powder to straining citrus juices and custards. Line a sieve with cheesecloth (muslin) to trap tiny seeds when straining fruit purées for making granitas.

## Saucepans

Ice cream custards and sauces are delicate mixtures, so any saucepan you use must heat evenly to avoid scorching. It must also not react with acidic ingredients or eggs. Stainless steel, anodized aluminum, and lined copper pans meet both criteria, making them good all-purpose choices. You will want to have a 1-quart (1-l) pan for melting butter and other small tasks, and a deep, narrow 2-quart (2-l) pan for making caramel and other hot sauces that can bubble up during cooking. A 3-quart (3-l) saucepan is ideal for cooking the custards for ice cream and gelato.

## Baking Pans

Metal baking pans are not limited to use in the oven, as many recipes in this book illustrate. An 8- or 9-inch (20- or 23-cm) square pan, for example, becomes a mold for ice cream bars. The large surface area of a shallow 9-by-13-inch (23-by-33-cm) pan simplifies freezing granitas. The removable sides of a springform pan make it a good choice for ice cream tortes. For variety, an 8½-by-4½-inch (21.5-by-11.5-cm) loaf pan can be used to create a rectangular-shaped torte.

You will need rimmed baking sheets for making Tuile Cookies (page 22) and Profiteroles (page 107), and a wire rack for cooling them. Plus, the baking sheets can do double duty as trays for holding all the little bowls for your *mise en place*. Finally, standard and miniature muffin pans make good molds for ice cream bon-bons or individual scoops.

## Brushes

Use a small pastry brush for moistening ladyfingers with liqueur or syrup, and use large brushes for the broad strokes needed for pound cake.

## Peelers and Graters

The large holes of a box grater-shredder are perfect for forming rough shavings of chocolate, while a rasp grater yields tiny shards of citrus zest. You can also use a rasp grater, such as a Microplane grater, for hard whole spices such as nutmeg (a specialized nutmeg grater, complete with a storage compartment, is also available). A swivel-bladed vegetable peeler is handy for removing citrus in wide strips and for forming beautiful chocolate curls.

## Thermometers

Instant-read thermometers and candy thermometers, each with a long stem topped by a face that registers the temperature, are used for testing custards and caramel. An oven thermometer (pictured center) that hangs from or sits on an oven rack allows you to monitor the accuracy of your oven.

## Miscellaneous

Citrus reamers make juicing citrus fruits easy, and pot holders (not pictured) are a must for handling hot pans. Your rolling pin is the right size for shaping warm Tuile Cookies (page 22), and the right heft for pounding nuts or nut brittle for sprinkling on top of ice cream sundaes. Popsicle sticks are used for ice cream or sorbet bars, and a pastry bag and a set of tips simplifies shaping *choux* pastry and adding whipped cream garnishes. A table fork is good for scraping granita or for coating ice cream balls with coconut or nuts. Finally, an inexpensive stove-top espresso maker is an easy way to brew espresso for coffee-flavored desserts.

## Storage Containers

You need tightly covered plastic storage containers for custards and sauces that are stored in the refrigerator and heavy-duty, freezer-safe versions of the same containers for freezing ice cream, gelato, sherbet, and sorbet. Containers with a capacity of 1 or 1½ quarts (1 or 1½ l) will accommodate most of the desserts in this book. Pack cookies and tortes in airtight, hardsided, heavy-duty plastic containers to protect them from crushing and to preserve their flavors.

## Ice Cream Scoops

Many different types of ice cream scoops are on the market. The simplest scoop is shaped like a shovel (not pictured), and its broad, thin edge yields rather flat layers when thrust into ice cream. It is especially helpful for smoothing out the layers in layered desserts. More traditional is a round scoop (sold in a wide variety of sizes) that uses either a spring-loaded mechanism or a nonstick finish to release the ice cream ball. Some scoops have a pointed end or a liquid concentration in the handle that heats the scoop which makes scooping very hard ice cream or sorbet easier. In every case, choose a high-quality scoop that won't break or buckle when used for solidly frozen desserts.

## Serving Items

Turn your kitchen into an old-fashioned soda fountain with all the serving dishes available for ice cream: elongated banana split bowls, footed parfait glasses, and tall ice cream glasses for malts, sodas, and milk shakes. Shot glasses and martini glasses are nice for serving granita. Small glass plates are perfect for plating composed desserts such as profiteroles or baked Alaskas. And be sure you have a variety of bowls on hand for simple scoops of ice cream; delicate clear glass ones are good for showing off the beauty of frozen desserts.

# Glossary

ALL-PURPOSE FLOUR Made from a blend of soft and hard wheat, all-purpose flour, also known as plain flour, is available bleached and unbleached. The latter has a slight ivory cast and a better flavor than the former, which has been chemically treated to produce a white color.

AMARETTO An almond-flavored liqueur traditionally made from herbs, fruits, and the oil of apricot pits—a flavor combination that pairs well with many fruit-based desserts and with chocolate. Though many distillers make amaretto, Amaretto di Saronno from Italy is considered the best.

ANISETTE A licorice-flavored liqueur made from aniseeds, anisette especially complements melon-based frozen desserts, such as Watermelon Granita (page 91).

APPLE CIDER This naturally sweetened beverage, also known as apple juice, is made from pressing the juice from apples. It is used in Green Apple Sorbet (page 87) to heighten the apple flavor.

BOURBON Distilled primarily from corn, this slightly sweet whiskey takes its name from a county in Kentucky where it is made.

BRANDY This familiar spirit is distilled primarily from fermented grape juice but also from other fruit juices. Eau-de-vie, grappa, and Cognac are all types of brandy.

BUTTER, UNSALTED Butter that is unsalted is preferable to salted because it tends to be fresher because salt acts as a preservative, lengthening the shelf life for butter at the supermarket. Refrigerate unsalted butter in its original wrapping for up to 6 weeks. Never use margarine, which can separate, preventing a sauce from becoming smooth and thick.

BUTTERMILK Traditionally, buttermilk is the liquid left behind when butter is churned from whole milk. Today, most buttermilk is cultured low-fat or nonfat milk, made by adding souring agents that turn the sugars to acids. Buttermilk has a longer refrigerator life than fresh milk.

CANOLA OIL Made from the seeds of the rape plant, a relative of the mustard plant, canola oil adds moisture without adding unwanted flavor to baked goods, such as Tuile Cookies (page 22), and gives melted chocolate a glossy sheen. Store in airtight bottles away from heat and light.

CARAMELIZE, TO To heat sugar until it melts and turns from light to dark brown, developing a more complex flavor. Sugar is caramelized when it registers between 320° and 350°F (160° and 180°C) on a candy thermometer. Caramelizing sugar is an important step in the making of Caramel Sauce (page 26).

CHOCOLATE
Originally from Central America but now cultivated in other equatorial regions, chocolate is produced by roasting and crushing cacao beans to produce "nibs," or kernels. The nibs are then pressed into a paste known as chocolate liquor. To store chocolate, tightly wrap it in aluminum foil and keep at cool room temperature. Dark chocolate will keep for up to 1 year; milk chocolate should be used within 3 months.

Chips Bittersweet and semisweet (plain) chips are firmer than milk or white chocolate chips, and tend to freeze solid, making large chunks hard to chew. Use mini-chips, which will begin to melt in the mouth more quickly, releasing their flavor and texture.

Cocoa powder When most of the cocoa butter is removed from chocolate liquor and the liquor is ground, unsweetened cocoa powder is the result. It is available in two types, regular and Dutch process. The latter is treated with an alkali solution, producing a milder flavor and darker color, and is preferred for the recipes in this book.

Dark Term used to describe any chocolate made from chocolate liquor sweetened with sugar and blended with additional cocoa butter but with no milk solids added. In general, European dark chocolates, which must contain at least 35 percent chocolate liquor, are called bittersweet, while American dark chocolates, which must contain at least 15 percent chocolate liquor, are called semisweet (plain).

Milk Made from chocolate liquor to which both sugar and milk solids have been added, milk chocolate is sweeter and softer than bittersweet or semisweet chocolate and should not be substituted for them.

White Made from cocoa butter, milk solids, sugar, and flavorings, white chocolate contains no chocolate liquor and is therefore not a true chocolate.

COCONUT Freshly grated or finely chopped fresh coconut meat (the white part) can be hard to find, and the flavor varies greatly from fruit to fruit. Flaked dried coconut sold in bags, bought in a store with good turnover, is more reliable. Most flaked coconut is sold sweetened, but an unsweetened version is available at specialty stores. Canned coconut milk separates, with the coconut "fat" rising to the top and becoming semisolid. Even if you buy reduced-fat, or "light," canned coconut milk, you will need to shake the can well before opening to recombine the liquid. Store leftover coconut milk in the refrigerator for about 3 days or freeze up to 1 month. Do not confuse canned unsweetened coconut milk with sweetened cream of coconut. Both are used in Coconut Ice Cream on page 53.

COPPER BOWL Copper chemically interacts with the albumin in egg whites, which helps them to stabilize and hold air better. Egg whites also increase in volume when they are beaten in a copper bowl. You do not need to add cream of tartar, which acts a stabilizer when using bowls made of other materials, and you should always transfer the whites to another bowl as soon as they are whipped. Copper bowls should not be used for mixtures that include acidic ingredients, such as lemon juice, as an off flavor will result.

CORE, TO To remove the central core, seeds, and/or stem from a fruit such as an apple or strawberry.

CORN SYRUP This syrup, made from corn starch, is a common commercial sweetener. Available in dark and light versions, corn syrup does not crystallize when heated.

COUPLER A small, two-piece plastic device made of a round grooved insert and a ring to tighten it, used for some pastry (piping) bags. The coupler makes it easy to change piping tips without changing pastry bags. It also prevents the contents of the bag from leaking out around the tip.

CRÈME DE CASSIS A type of liqueur that is black currant–flavored, it pairs well with stone fruits such as plums.

CRÈME DE MENTHE This mint-flavored liqueur is available as either a clear or a green liquid. The two types can be used interchangeably, though the green version will impart color as well as flavor.

CREAM, HEAVY Also known as heavy whipping cream, whipping cream, and double cream, heavy cream is high in butterfat (at least 36 percent) and has a rich flavor. Do not substitute light cream or half-and-half for the heavy cream called for in the recipes in this book. Avoid purchasing ultrapasteurized cream, which has been heated to extend its shelf life and does not whip as fully when used for whipped cream.

CREAM OF TARTAR This powdery, white substance, technically known as potassium tartrate, is a by-product of wine making. It stabilizes and promotes volume when whipping egg whites.

CUSTARD A cooked mixture of eggs and milk and/or cream that is heated just until the proteins in the ingredients thicken to form a soft, smooth, satiny base for ice creams and gelatos.

EGGS Eggs are sometimes used uncooked in meringues and other preparations. Although the incidence of salmonella or other bacteria in eggs is statistically extremely low, many cooks believe precautions must be taken. This risk is greatest to young children, elders, pregnant women, and anyone with a compromised immune system. If you have health and safety concerns, do not consume raw eggs. In some cases, pasteurized egg products can replace them. To store, leave eggs in their original carton and store in the refrigerator. Use them by the sell-by date stamped on the package.

ESPRESSO If a recipe calls for brewed espresso or ground espresso-roast beans, buy whole beans from a good coffee shop and grind them at home to use for brewing or for adding to a custard base. Or, have them ground at the store but ideally use within 12 hours of purchase, before the natural oils begin to dissipate.

EXTRACTS Concentrated flavorings made from plants, extracts—also called essences—are used to flavor many frozen desserts. The most common extracts used in this book are vanilla and almond. Pure vanilla extract is made by steeping vanilla beans, preferably Bourbon-Madagascar or Tahitian, in alcohol to extract their flavor; pure almond extract is based on oil of bitter almond. Never use imitation flavorings, which can lend a chemical taste.

FRUIT

Fruits provide a variety of flavorings for all kinds of frozen desserts. For the best results, buy the freshest, in-season fruits that you can find.

Apple Choose tart, green varieties such as Granny Smith or pippin for the most intense apple flavor. Look for firm fruits with good color and no soft spots.

Banana Unlike most fruits, bananas are available year-round. Though picked and shipped while still green and unripe, most bananas ripen beautifully when left at room temperature. If bananas ripen before you are ready to use them, refrigerate them to retard the ripening process. The skins will turn black, but the fruit inside will be fine.

Grapefruit The pulp of this large, popular citrus can range from white to pale pink to red, depending on the variety. For ease, look for one of the many seedless varieties.

Lemon This small citrus fruit was first cultivated in tropical regions of Asia and India before the Moors introduced it to Europe. Today, the most popular varieties found in grocery stores are Eureka and Lisbon. The less-common Meyer lemon has softer pulp, a sweeter flavor, and a floral fragrance. Choose lemons heavy for their size and free of blemishes or soft spots.

Lime Smaller and more delicate than lemons, limes are tart with a hint of sweetness. The Persian, available year-round, is the most common grocery-store variety; smaller, rounder, extremely tart Key limes, at their seasonal peak in late spring or early summer, are harder to find. If necessary, frozen or bottled Key lime juice can be used in place of freshly squeezed juice.

Mango First grown in India and now cultivated in other tropical regions, this fragrant, oval fruit has skin that ranges from green to pale yellow or orange and flesh that is light to deep yellow. Choose fruits that give slightly to light pressure and are fragrant near the stem end.

Melon Many melon varieties exist, but they can generally be divided into two broad categories: muskmelons (such as cantaloupe and honeydew) and watermelons. Avoid refrigerating uncut melons; they will absorb odors and the cold will inhibit their flavor development. Instead, buy ripe melons and use right away or store on the counter for no more than a day. When buying a watermelon, look for a large, pale yellow (but not white, soft, or moldy) patch on one side; this indicates that the watermelon was left on the vine longer and will be sweeter.

Orange First grown in China, oranges are now cultivated around the world. Choose unblemished fruits that feel heavy for their size and have shiny skin, which indicates the natural citrus oils are still present.

Peach Ripe peaches are fragile and can easily bruise, so growers sometimes pick them early, when the fruit is sturdy but unripe. Though peaches can ripen off the tree, they will never develop the intoxicating perfume or buttery texture of a tree-ripened fruit, so always purchase them ripe, if possible.

Plum Depending on the variety, the skin and flesh color of this popular stone fruit ranges from yellow and green to many shades of pink, purple, and scarlet. In general, smaller plums are more acidic and better for cooking than the larger, juicier varieties.

Raspberry Supermarket raspberries are often lacking in flavor. If you can't find good-flavored, fresh berries, frozen unsweetened raspberries are a better choice. Always strain out the tiny seeds from raspberry purée before using it for flavoring an ice cream or sorbet base.

Strawberry Choose firm, deep red berries with lush green leaves and no pale or white patches around the stem. Small to medium strawberries are usually more flavorful than giant ones. Just before using, rinse the whole berries with leaves attached in cool water, then pat dry with paper towels. If rinsed earlier or with leaves removed, the berries will absorb water, which will turn them mushy and dilute their flavor.

GRAND MARNIER This is the grande dame of orange-flavored liqueurs, which also include Cointreau, Curaçao, and Triple Sec. It is made by flavoring brandy with bitter orange peel, vanilla, and spices and is typically sipped over ice when not being used—always sparingly—as a flavoring for a wide variety of desserts.

GRATE, TO To render a food into tiny particles, usually by rubbing it over the sharp, pointy rasps on a box grater-shredder or a rasp grater. Typically done so that an ingredient, such as citrus zest, more easily blends into a mixture.

KAHLÚA A popular and distinctive Mexican coffee liqueur flavored with herbs and vanilla. Pairs well with chocolate- or espresso-flavored frozen desserts.

MACERATE, TO To soak a food, such as the mint leaves in Mint–Chocolate Chip Ice Cream (page 62), in sugar and/or a flavorful liquid, such as liqueur, to enhance its flavor and sometimes soften its texture.

MARSALA A fortified wine traditionally made near the Sicilian city of the same name, rich-tasting, amber Marsala is available in sweet and dry forms.

MARSHMALLOWS Fluffy white treats made from corn syrup, gelatin, sugar, and other flavorings, marshmallows are often used for their flavor and soft texture. Marshmallows exposed to air dry out and harden relatively quickly. Use fresh, soft marshmallows for ice creams; they will have enough moisture to remain chewy and soft, rather than freeze solid. Also called fluff.

MASCARPONE A soft, rich cow's milk cream cheese that originated in Italy's Lombardy region. Look for mascarpone in small tubs in the cheese section of the grocery store. Once opened, it should be used within a few days.

MERINGUE Sweet, white, and fluffy, this delicate mixture is produced by beating together egg whites and sugar. A soft, glossy, smooth meringue is used for covering Individual Baked Alaskas (page 113), a classic frozen dessert.

MILK The rich flavor of whole milk comes from its emulsified fats, its distinctive white color derives from casein protein, and its faintly sweet flavor reveals the presence of lactose, a type of sugar found only in milk and its by-products. Almost all milk sold today is homogenized, which means that it has been forced through tiny holes to break its fat globules into small particles that will remain suspended evenly throughout the liquid. Be sure to use low-fat or whole milk for the recipes in this book. Nonfat milk will not yield the desired rich result.

MINT The most common mints available in markets or grown in home gardens are peppermint, which is relatively pungent and has small, bright green leaves and purple stems, and spearmint, which is milder and has grayish green leaves. Either one, or another variety, can be used. Rinse mint leaves briefly under running water shortly before using; if left to sit, the leaves will turn brown and lose their potency.

MOLASSES A syrup that can be used as a sweetener for some frozen desserts such as Pumpkin Ice Cream (page 65). Molasses is a by-product of sugar refinement, a process that requires boiling cane syrup. Use light molasses for the recipes in this book.

NONSTICK COOKING SPRAY Available in a variety of types, including canola oil, olive oil, and vegetable oil, nonstick cooking spray is canned oil packed under pressure, dispersed by a propellant, and used to grease baking sheets and other cooking surfaces.

NUTS

Nuts provide both flavor and texture to many frozen desserts. They have a high oil content, which means they can turn rancid easily, so proper storage is critical. Pack nuts in tightly capped glass jars, airtight plastic containers, or locking plastic bags and store in the refrigerator for up to 3 months or in the freezer for up to 6 months.

Almonds Found inside the pits of a dried fruit related to the peach, these oval nuts are delicate and fragrant and have a smooth texture. They are sold both unblanched, with their natural brown skins intact, and blanched, with the skins removed to reveal their light ivory color.

Peanuts These popular nuts, which are concealed inside of a waffle-veined pod rather than a shell, are actually not nuts at all, but are instead a type of legume that grows on underground stems.

Pecans A native of North America, the pecan is a member of the hickory family, and has two crinkled lobes of nutmeat, much like its relative, the walnut. Hundreds of varieties exist, but they all have smooth, brown, oval shells that break easily. Their flavor is sweeter and more delicate than walnuts.

Pistachios Used widely in Mediterranean, Middle Eastern, and Indian cuisines and as an addition to ice cream or gelato (page 69), the pistachio has a thin, hard shell that is creamy tan and rounded. As the nut ripens, its shell cracks to reveal a light green kernel inside. Bright red nuts owe their color to vegetable dye.

Walnuts The furrowed, double-lobed nutmeat of the walnut has an assertive, rich flavor. The most common variety is the English walnut, also known as the Persian walnut, which has a light brown shell that cracks easily. Black walnuts have a stronger flavor and extremely hard shells but are a challenge to find.

ORANGE-FLOWER WATER Made by distilling the blossoms of the bitter orange, this aromatic water is used to flavor ice cream, gelato, and other frozen desserts.

PARCHMENT PAPER Treated to withstand the high heat of an oven, parchment paper is ideal for lining rimmed baking sheets. Also known as baking paper, it resists moisture and grease and has a smooth nonstick surface. Look for parchment paper in well-stocked markets and cookware shops.

PIPE, TO To make decorative effects or shaped forms by spooning whipped cream or a batter into the wide end of a pastry (piping) bag and then forcing, or piping, it out of the bag's narrow tip.

POMEGRANATE JUICE Extracted from pomegranate seeds, this bright red juice is stocked in the fresh-juice section of many markets and health-food stores and is available by mail order.

ROSE WATER Made by distilling rose petals, rose water has an intense flavor and fragrance. It can be used to flavor ice cream, gelato, and other frozen desserts.

RUM, DARK Distilled from sugarcane juice or molasses, this Caribbean liquor comes in many different colors, from milk white or silver to gold, amber, dark, and Demerara, the darkest. As the color darkens, the flavor becomes stronger.

SCOTCH A type of whiskey that is made only in Scotland. Unlike American whiskeys, which are made from corn, Scotch whiskey is made from barley. In this book, it is used for Butterscotch Sauce (page 28).

SILICONE BAKING LINER Increasingly popular, silicone pan liners help prevent baked goods, such as Tuile Cookies (page 22), from sticking and from overbrowning.

SPICES
Essential oils are the source of flavor in spices, but they will dissipate over time, so replace your spices periodically. Purchase spices in small amounts from stores with high turnover and label them with the date of purchase. For the best flavor, use whole spices and grind them fresh when they are needed. If stored in closed airtight containers in a cool, dark place, ground spices will keep for about 6 months and whole spices for about 1 year.

Allspice The berry of an evergreen tree, allspice tastes like a combination of cinnamon, nutmeg, and cloves.

Cinnamon This popular rust-colored spice, appreciated for its warm, sweet flavor, is the bark of a tropical evergreen tree. It is sold both as sticks and ground.

Cloves Shaped like a small nail with a round head, the almost-black clove is the dried bud of a tropical evergreen tree. It has a strong, sweet flavor.

Ginger Fragrant and flavorful, this knobby rhizome, or underground stem, has a spicy-sweet flavor. It is available fresh, ground, and crystallized (candied in sugar syrup and then coated with granulated sugar).

Nutmeg The small oval brown seed of a soft fruit, a nutmeg has a hard shell covered by a membrane that is removed, dried, and then marketed as mace, another distinctive spice. Whole nutmeg keeps its warm, sweet flavor longer than ground, and can be grated as needed with a special nutmeg or other fine rasp grater.

SUGAR
A variety of sugars are used in frozen desserts. For the recipes in this book, buy sugar that is labeled "cane sugar," as sugar made from sugar beets can have an unpredictable effect when used for making frozen desserts. Keep all types of sugars in tightly covered airtight containers in a clean, dry place. They will last indefinitely.

Brown Rich in flavor, brown sugar is granulated sugar colored with molasses. It has a soft, moist texture and comes in two main types, milder-flavored light brown and stronger-flavored dark brown. Never expose it to the open air for an extended period, or the moisture will evaporate and the sugar will clump and harden.

Confectioners' Also known as powdered or icing sugar, confectioners' sugar is simply granulated sugar that has been crushed to a powder and mixed with a little cornstarch (cornflour) to prevent caking. In this book, it is mainly used for sprinkling on finished desserts, such as Profiteroles (page 107).

Granulated Granulated white sugar is the most commonly used sugar. The size of the granules varies with the manufacturer. For easy dissolving, look for granules that are not too large.

TEMPER, TO To heat beaten eggs slightly before adding them to hot liquid, in order to keep them from curdling. When making a custard base for ice cream and gelato, the eggs must be tempered before mixing them with the hot cream mixture.

VANILLA BEANS The fruit of an orchid plant, vanilla beans differ widely in flavor depending on the region and growing conditions of the bean. When choosing vanilla beans, Tahitian beans have the most subtle flavor, while beans from Madagascar have a pronounced flavor. Look for long, glossy, soft, plump beans with a strong aroma. Store in a resealable plastic bag or a jar with a tight lid away from moisture and direct light.

WHIPPING The process of beating a food, such as heavy (double) cream or egg whites, to increase its volume by incorporating air into it. Whipped ingredients are sometimes used to lighten the texture of heavier mixtures, such as folding whipped cream into the base for a frozen soufflé (page 101).

ZEST The outer colored portion of the citrus peel, which is rich in flavorful oils. Only remove the colored portion and not the bitter white pith underneath. When choosing citrus for zesting, look for organic fruit, as pesticides concentrate in the peel.

# Index

**FREE PRESS**

A Division of Simon & Schuster, Inc.
1230 Avenue of the Americas
New York, NY 10020

**WILLIAMS-SONOMA**

Founder & Vice-Chairman  Chuck Williams

**WELDON OWEN INC.**

Chief Executive Officer  John Owen
President and Chief Operating Officer  Terry Newell
Chief Financial Officer  Christine E. Munson
Vice President International Sales  Stuart Laurence
Creative Director  Gaye Allen
Publisher  Hannah Rahill
Senior Editor  Jennifer Newens
Associate Editor  Donita Boles
Art Director  Kyrie Forbes
Designers  Adrienne Aquino and Andrea Stephany
Production Director  Chris Hemesath
Color Manager  Teri Bell
Production and Reprint Coordinator  Todd Rechner
Food Stylist  Alison Attenborough
Prop Stylist  Nancy Micklin Thomas
Assistant Food Stylist  Colin Flynn
Assistant Food Stylist and Hand Model  Katie Christ
Photographer's Assistant  Amy Sessler

**PHOTO CREDITS**

Mark Thomas, all photography, except the following:
Bill Bettencourt: page 36, page 37 (chocolate curls).
Tucker & Hossler: page 39.

**THE MASTERING SERIES**

Conceived and produced by Weldon Owen Inc.
814 Montgomery Street, San Francisco, CA 94133
Telephone: 415 291 0100 Fax: 415 291 8841

In collaboration with Williams-Sonoma, Inc.
3250 Van Ness Avenue, San Francisco, CA 94109

A WELDON OWEN PRODUCTION
Copyright © 2006 by Weldon Owen Inc. and Williams-Sonoma Inc.

All rights reserved, including the right of reproduction in whole or in part in any form.

FREE PRESS and colophon are registered trademarks of Simon & Schuster, Inc.

For information regarding special discounts for bulk purchases, please contact Simon & Schuster Special Sales at 1 800 456 6798 or business@simonandschuster.com

Set in ITC Berkeley and FF The Sans.

Color separations by Embassy Graphics.
Printed and bound in China by SNP Leefung Printers Limited.

First printed in 2006.

10 9 8 7 6 5 4 3 2 1

Library of Congress Cataloging-in-Publication data is available.

ISBN–13: 978-0-7432-7106-6
ISBN–10: 0-7432-7106-8

**ACKNOWLEDGMENTS**

Weldon Owen wishes to thank the following people for their generous support in producing this book: Ken DellaPenta, Lisa Ekström, Leslie Evans, Arin Hailey, Sharon Silva, and Sharron Wood.

**A NOTE ON WEIGHTS AND MEASURES**

All recipes include customary U.S. and metric measurements. Metric conversions are based on a standard developed for these books and have been rounded off. Actual weights may vary.